# COMMUNICATION
## and
# CULTURE

## A Guide for Practice

### Cynthia Gallois
*The University of Queensland, Australia*

### Victor J. Callan
*The University of Queensland, Australia*

JOHN WILEY & SONS

Chichester · New York · Weinheim · Brisbane · Singapore · Toronto

*Other Wiley Editorial Offices*

John Wiley & Sons, Inc., 605 Third Avenue,
New York, NY 10158-0012, USA

VCH Verlagsgesellschaft mbH, Pappelallee 3,
0-69469 Weinheim, Germany

Jacaranda Wiley Ltd, 33 Park Road, Milton,
Queensland 4064, Australia

John Wiley & Sons (Asia) Pte Ltd, 2 Clementi Loop #02-01,
Jin Xing Distripark, Singapore 129809

John Wiley & Sons (Canada) Ltd, 22 Worcester Road,
Rexdale, Ontario M9W 1L1, Canada

*Library of Congress Cataloging-in-Publication Data*

Gallois, Cynthia.
    Communication and culture : a guide for practice / Cynthia
Gallois, Victor J. Callan.
        p.    cm. — (Wiley series in culture and professional practice)
    Includes bibliographical references and index.
    ISBN 0-471-96622-3 (pbk.)
    1. Intercultural communication.   2. Communication and culture.
I. Callan, Victor J., 1954–    II. Title.   III. Series.
GN345.6.G37   1997
303.48'2—dc20                                              96-42121
                                                              CIP

*British Library Cataloguing in Publication Data*

A catalogue record for this book is available from the British Library

ISBN 0-471-96622-3

Typeset in 11/13pt Palatino by Dorwyn Ltd, Rowlands Castle, Hants
Printed and bound in Great Britain by Biddles Ltd, Guildford
This book is printed on acid-free paper responsibly manufactured from sustainable
forestation, for which at least two trees are planted for each one used for paper
production.

# CONTENTS

# ABOUT THE AUTHORS

*Cynthia Gallois* received her PhD from the University of Florida. She joined the Psychology Department at The University of Queensland in 1979, and is now Professor of Psychology there. She has a long-term research and teaching interest in intercultural and intergroup communication, especially with respect to ethnicity, gender, organisational status, and sexual orientation. This interest has led her to study the combined impact of assertive communication, communication accommodation, and social rules on intergroup communication. She is also involved in research and teaching about human sexuality, particularly prevention of HIV and other STDs and HIV-related discrimination. She has published several books and a large number of book chapters and journal articles in these areas. She is currently Editor of *Human Communication Research*. She is active in professional associations in communication and psychology, and is now the President of the Society of Australasian Social Psychologists.

*Victor J. Callan* received his PhD from the University of New South Wales, and joined The University of Queensland in 1979. He is now Professor and Head of the Graduate School of Management. He has published several books in the areas of social, health and cross-cultural psychology, and over 100 book chapters and journal articles in international publications. He has spent over 17 years studying how interpersonal communication is influenced by social, cultural and, more recently, organisational factors. He also consults and workshops in the area of communication in the workplace to public and private sector organisations. He has long been active in professional associations in management, organisational psychology, and cross-cultural psychology.

The two authors have worked as a team in the area of intergroup communication since their first semester at The University of Queensland. Their work has appeared frequently in books and journals in social psychology, cross-cultural psychology, communication, and management. Their current research explores the influence of group membership, including culture, on communication in the workplace.

# SERIES PREFACE

The Wiley Series in Culture and Professional Practice provides a guide for professionals whose daily work in a number of fields requires them to consider the role of cultural factors in the needs and behaviour of their clients.

Whether through immigration, urbanisation, the aftermath of wars and natural disasters, the movement of people around the world in the large multinational business organisations, or even the world-wide development of tourist travel, few are untouched by contact with people of cultures different from their own. Professional help is often called for, but too often professional training courses do not give much consideration to cultural issues. The volumes in this Series will offer some practical help for these situations.

The Series covers some of the most frequent professional situations in which culture is an important influence.

I. *Culture and the Child* deals with issues in child care and development. Topics include temperamental and behavioural differences, the family, social interactions, children's motivations and anxieties and dealing with children in multicultural social contexts.

II. *Culture and Communication* deals with problems of communicating in business and interactions in many different settings.

III. *Culture and Community Health* shows how different cultural orientations impact upon concepts of health and illness and so affect how professionals and patients can relate to each other for better understanding and health care.

IV. *Culture and Education* deals with schooling and the learning problems of children from cultural minorities within national schooling systems, but also sympathetically addresses the problems from the point of view of the difficult task of school administrators.

V. *Culture and the Law* takes up the different perceptions of culturally differing groups toward the legal system and the consequences in the legal processes.

Each volume in the Series has been written by an expert in the field who has had extensive experience in working with people of different cultures. Each has also carried out cross-cultural research in the field.

The books in the Series are designed for everyday use so have been deliberately kept to a modest size. They are intended to complement the accepted texts in the field and all assume the basic professional knowledge of practitioners in the field. Students in professional training programmes and participants in in-service development courses should also find these books helpful.

# ACKNOWLEDGEMENTS

We began doing research together on intercultural communication in 1979. Since that time, we have been helped by colleagues and students too numerous to name individually, many of whom appear on the publications referred to in this book, and without whom the research would not have been possible. We are very grateful to them and to the many people from Australian and other cultural groups who have participated in the research. Many of the ideas in this book were sharpened during the course of workshops and courses we have conducted at The University of Queensland and elsewhere, and we thank the participants in them for their questions and their fresh perspectives. During the course of writing the book, we appreciated very much the help of Nicole Gillespie and Matthew Jones with references and Katy White with the index, as well as the patience and forbearance of Debbie Terry, John Gardner, and especially Jeff Pittam, for keeping the research projects and the rest of life going. We are very grateful for the helpful comments of the series editor, Daphne Keats, and for the unfailing support of Michael Coombs, Wendy Hudlass, Comfort Jegede, and Mike Shardlow at Wiley. Finally, we would like to remember Luke Jones, who was a constant reminder of how to keep your perspective in adverse circumstances, and who made very good intuitive use of the ideas in this book.

Cindy Gallois
Victor Callan
*Brisbane, 1996*

# 1

# INTRODUCTION: THE CHALLENGE OF INTERCULTURAL COMMUNICATION

This is a book for professional and business people who deal with other people from various backgrounds and social groups and in particular from different cultures. Of course, it could be said that this book applies to every professional person, as intercultural contact is becoming the *sine qua non* in both private and public business today. In the past, many people lived in their villages, leaving intergroup interaction to politicians and kings, warriors, and long-distance traders (who were often members of nomadic or trader cultures themselves). In this century, the isolated village has largely come to an end, to be replaced for many of us by the global village, as Marshall McLuhan (1964) called it. Not only are we increasingly likely to interact face-to-face with people from other cultures (not to mention other sub-cultural groups), but it is almost inevitable that we will communicate with them by telephone, by fax, or on the internet.

Sometimes, the way to successful intercultural communication is very smooth. There are many stories of intercultural friendships (professional and personal) developing on the internet, and a large number of tales of deals abroad successfully completed. In addition, many of us know people who seem to have a knack for dealing with those from other cultures; they can 'get into the skin' of members of the other group without losing sight of their own, or of the task at hand. These people can be and often are excellent guides for colleagues—but how do they do it?

At other times, the road is anything but smooth. Somehow, misunderstandings occur, people give the wrong impression, and anger, frustration, and intolerance develop. What is especially relevant to this book is that such scenarios are frequently played out without people from either culture knowing how it started, what the other person did (or what they themselves did) that was so wrong. Instead, a series of small misunderstandings or violations of rules may actually have gone unchallenged at the time, but led to growing resentment and anger that burst out for no apparent reason (see Tannen, 1986). In some cases, on the other hand, one person or more is well aware of what has gone wrong, even though that person may not be willing to speak about it: someone from the other culture has done something outrageous. It goes without saying (in the opinion of the first person) that the other person, and very probably everyone else from this culture, is reprehensible (see Hall, 1959). But *why* was what the other person did so wrong—that may be harder to describe. In yet other cases, the interaction seems to be doomed almost from the start, because prejudice by one or both sides means there is no latitude for error—every tiny mistake is magnified and interpreted in the worst possible light.

In the face of both their good and their bad experiences, business and professional people through necessity have developed skills in intergroup and intercultural communication. This book represents an attempt to apply the results of many years of research in cross-cultural psychology (particularly cross-cultural social psychology) to making this task more systematic and more efficient. We will emphasise four main areas where, we believe, the methods, theory, and research results of cross-cultural psychology and communication aid in smoothing the way:

— social identity and prejudice
— values and rules clarification
— perspective-taking
— communication strategies.

Before looking at the ways of handling difficult intercultural situations, we will spend the rest of this chapter highlighting some of the problems that arise again and again in intercultural encounters.

## MISUNDERSTANDING PEOPLE FROM OTHER CULTURES

### Misunderstandings Based on Language

An obvious problem area when two people from different cultures communicate is language. Language is not a problem for everybody; indeed the majority of the world's people are bilingual or multilingual. In the business community, this is becoming increasingly the case, especially as business people realise that the 'language of business is the customer's language, whatever language that is'. In many parts of the world, people have developed the custom of using different languages for different purposes, a practice called *diglossia*. For example, Fishman (1971a), describes an office scene in Puerto Rico where the boss and his secretary, both of whom are native Puerto Ricans of Hispanic ethnicity, discuss work-related matters in English, switch to Spanish to chat about their weekend activities, and switch back to English to continue working. Interestingly enough, the boss initiates the language switches, and the secretary follows his lead; we will discuss subtle displays of power like this in a later chapter. In a diglossic or multiglossic environment, everyone is likely to have the requisite language competency. Even so, some people, particularly foreigners who have learned the languages outside the culture, may get into trouble about which language to use in which context.

There are many intercultural situations, however, where one person cannot speak the other's language adequately to do the task at hand. This situation is especially common where native speakers of English are involved, as people of British and American ethnic background are among the largest groups of monolingual speakers in the world. It is also common in countries with active immigration, like the United States, Canada, Australia, and increasingly the countries of Western Europe. In these countries, immigrants may come in to work with no knowledge of the native language at all, and pick up the language in crash courses and on the streets.

Native speakers, when confronted with an employee, colleague, or customer who seems to have an inadequate command of the language, tend to experience frustration, often coupled with resentment and anger ('Why can't people who live and work here at least learn the language? Why do I have to waste my time trying to communicate with them?'). In our own research, we have found that once native speakers of Australian English hear a foreign accent in English, they tune out instead of listening carefully—why bother to listen, if it's so hard (Gallois & Callan, 1986)? These feelings can lead to ineffective ways of dealing with the problem, like speaking louder and louder. Another unfortunate result is 'foreigner talk', speech in which language is degraded, like baby talk, supposedly to make it simpler. The following example, taken from our own experience, illustrates foreigner talk:

COLLEAGUE A: B, could you take the report up to Mr C asap?

COLLEAGUE B: Sorry—I don't understand.

COLLEAGUE A: Could you please take the report up to Mr C asap??? (*said louder this time*)

COLLEAGUE B: You want that I finish the report?

COLLEAGUE A: B—TO TAKE—REPORT—MR C—RIGHT AWAY!

COLLEAGUE B: Sorry?

As you can see, A's use of foreigner talk has made the request (command) to B harder to understand than it initially was, even for a native speaker, and it initially contained jargon— 'asap'—which B could hardly be expected to know and which was not changed to plain English until the third try. Foreigner talk may satisfy (temporarily) the anger of a native speaker, but it does nothing to aid communication. Yet it can be very hard to resist. Indeed, we have the habit of this kind of talk because we commonly use it with young children and animals—and to the elderly, which is not very appropriate either.

Language-based misunderstandings can arise, of course, even when two native speakers of the same language, but from different dialect groups (e.g., Americans and British) or from different sub-cultures (e.g., European Americans and African Americans) or social classes, interact. There are a plethora of examples of words and phrases that mean subtly different things, or completely different things in one dialect and another; think of 'lift', 'boot', 'it went down like a bomb', 'knock up', 'cheers', 'you're right', 'no fear', in British, American, and Australian English, to name but a few. To these problems, add all the ones that come from people in one dialect group (or, in some cases, professional or occupational group) using words or phrases which people in another simply do not know, such as technical terms, jargon, slang, and 'big words', can throw the best intentioned intergroup communicators off the rails. The situation is made worse because the people involved often believe there should be no problem—after all, they 'speak the same language', don't they?

An example of how subtle and ubiquitous this process of misunderstanding can be comes from a recent personal experience. One of us was in the USA, visiting a number of organisations and giving talks there. In one of them, I received some rather sharp questioning about my work, and I defended myself as politely and as elegantly as I could. One pointed question, from a rather aggressive American colleague (who, as it happened, was a long-time friend), seemed well-justified, and I wanted to let him know that I realised it. So I answered, 'Fair comment, but . . .' and went on to give my defence. He looked a bit surprised, but said nothing, so I pressed on. Later on, he said to me, 'I didn't know how to take your remark, "fair comment". First I thought you meant my comment was worth a 3 on a scale where 1 is poor and 5 is good. Then I remembered you Aussies are always saying strange things, and I decided you must mean something else.' At least he gave me the benefit of the doubt, even if it was at the expense of a slight cultural slur.

The kinds of misunderstandings described above seem the most obvious examples of intercultural communication breakdown, but in many ways they are the easiest to deal with—partly because they *are* so obvious. In addition, if two people cannot understand each other's language, then interpreters can be brought in (although this solution brings its own challenges), or one or both people can learn the foreign language, if they are willing to do so. Sometimes, of course, a language-based problem comes not from lack of knowledge or ability to speak the other language, but from an unwillingness to do so (see Ryan & Giles, 1982, for a detailed description of this situation). For instance, speakers of Flemish in Belgium during the 1960s and 1970s, and, more recently, speakers of French in Canada, have refused on occasions to use or to learn the other language of the country (French and English, respectively) as part of a cultural and political protest. We will have more to say about language attitudes in later chapters. As we will see, such an unwillingness to accommodate can extend beyond language to dialect, vocabulary, and style, and can be an important signal of the relations between two cultural groups.

## Misunderstandings Based in Non-verbal Behaviour

Language is accompanied by a continuous flow of non-verbal communication, which involves not only the voice (the pitch, tone, speed, and quality of speech) but also the face (gaze, facial expression) and the body (the distance we stand from others, our spatial orientation to them, posture, gesture, touch, and the like). Even though some types of non-verbal behaviour appear to be innate, cultures differ greatly in their use of this behaviour and in their beliefs about what is appropriate. Thus, another major source of misunderstandings occurs on the non-verbal channels. For example, a Japanese man may believe that Americans are excitable and emotional because they speak loudly, while the American he is talking to thinks he is reserved and inscrutable because he speaks softly and his face moves relatively little when they converse. Beyond this, we can misinterpret what the behaviour means. For example, the smile on the face of a Japanese businessman, or kamikaze pilot during the Second World War, does not necessarily convey amusement or happiness; smiling in Japan is also strongly associated with nervousness, social discomfort, or, in some cases, even extreme sorrow.

Misunderstandings based in differences in non-verbal behaviour can be very hard to detect, because much of this behaviour is produced and received outside of conscious awareness. As we will see later, non-verbal behaviour functions largely to express emotion, mood, identity, and attitude in conversation, while words carry most of the ideas and facts. Thus, often we feel that only the words matter. This is particularly so in the West, where cultural values place more credence in words than in the non-verbal signals that accompany them. For this reason, it is easy to deny non-verbal behaviour, and equally easy not to pay attention to it. The following kind of exchange is commonplace in many Western countries:

COLLEAGUE A (*using a loud voice, with strong emphasis on each word, with a frown, and leaning hard towards the other person*): 'IS THE REPORT DONE *YET?*

COLLEAGUE B: Why are you so aggressive—I only got the assignment yesterday—no need to shout!

COLLEAGUE A (*calmly and neutrally*): All I did was ask whether the report was done yet—don't get so hot under the collar.

In fact, this kind of thing is so common that many books on assertive communication distinguish between assertion and aggression, or between various types of assertion (e.g., empathic assertion or assertion with understanding, as against ordinary assertion) mainly in terms of non-verbal behaviour (see Wilson & Gallois, 1993). The impact of non-verbal behaviour may also explain why many people, both Western and Eastern, find it difficult to distinguish between assertive communication and aggression. In many cases, the difference is mainly in the way the message is delivered; that is, in non-verbal behaviour.

Those of us who interact frequently with people from different cultures are usually aware of one aspect of non-verbal behaviour where cultures and sub-cultures differ: the meaning of emblematic gestures. Strictly speaking, such gestures are a type of verbal behaviour, because they substitute directly for words. For example, in American English, running the index finger in small circles around the temple means, 'He's crazy', or 'It's a crazy idea'. Quite a lot of these gestures are suggestive or obscene (one reason, perhaps, that they are gestures rather than words), which means that they may be quite acceptable in one country, but mean something different and unacceptable in another: the American V-for-victory sign, which is obscene in Europe, is the classic example. In other cases, the meaning stays clean from one language to another, but changes greatly. For example, the French use the gesture of pulling their lower eyelid with the index finger as a sign of disbelief ('my eye'), while in Iran, the same gesture means 'I promise' (but is also translated as 'my eye'). Researchers have gone to great lengths to construct cross-cultural dictionaries of such emblems; one of the best examples is Morris et al.'s (1979) dictionary of emblems in European languages, which gives the scope of each gesture and indicates the small ways in which emblems change from one community to another.

Once again, it is not the most obvious cases that are the most difficult; rather, it is the subtle differences in non-verbal behaviour which really get in the way. A well-studied example (see Hall, 1966), which we will deal with in more detail later, is the distance at which we stand when conversing with another person. The spectacle of the Englishman being backed around a room by an Arab (the Englishman is trying to get more distance while the Arab tries to get closer), and the analogous scene of an American backing a Japanese around the room for the same reason, is the stuff of many intercultural travellers' nightmares. One reason for this is that the traveller may not be able to put a finger on what is wrong. For some reason, thinks the traveller, the other person is backing off (or is crowding me)—I don't know how, and I don't know why, but I don't like it. The traveller (and the other person) may not realise that he or she has strong beliefs about where to stand. They may even think that little things like this do not matter at all—what counts is the words you say, being honest, and getting on with the business at hand. Unfortunately, contretemps on the non-verbal channels can prevent the business being done at all.

## Misunderstandings Based in Differences in Style, Conventions, and Practices

So far, we have pointed to some communication problems which stem from the micro-level features of communication. Another level of communication involves more large-scale features. One of these is the *style* in which we speak, including the *register*, or type of language, we adopt. All of us have a repertoire of styles which we can draw upon, ranging from the very formal and ritualised styles used in courtrooms, churches, and a few other places (increasingly few in English) through to the most intimate and informal language and behaviour we use with our family, closest friends, and perhaps our pet animals (see Joos, 1962). We use these styles in different contexts and for different purposes—this is the same kind of process as diglossia, except that it stays within the confines of a single language. Language register is similar to style, and refers to the specialised communication practices adopted in different contexts: business language is a good example of register. In our native language, we usually have a fairly sophisticated grasp of style; for example, in Australia we know not to address a judge with, 'G'day, mate', and not to call a friend 'Your honour'. While this seems blatantly obvious to the initiated, it is interesting that some people, including children, are exempt from many style conventions because they cannot be expected to have learned them.

Once again, cultures are different in their rules about which style and register to use in which context. Chinese and Japanese, for example, have a wider and more complex range of formal styles than English. In addition, in these languages the relationship of the speakers, including age, sex, and status, is clearly marked by the use of different words and parts of words, while in English, relationship is expressed more vaguely, in the way sentences are put together, who speaks more, and the like. English is even vague about what to call people in many contexts—for example, when do you start to call your supervisor 'John' instead of 'Mr Smith'? How do you know that you should make the switch? We will discuss rules about forms of address later. What all this means is that speakers of European languages have to master a set of words and phrases in Japanese, if they learn the language, that all seem to mean the same thing—then they are in doubt about which to use. For Japanese and Chinese learning Western languages, the learning task appears easier, until they find themselves in conversation with a stranger and literally do not know what to say.

In fact, one of the most difficult tasks for foreigners in learning a new language is learning the different styles and the contexts in which they are used. Many fluent speakers never manage this, and tend to speak in a single style, which makes them sound too formal in some contexts and too chatty in others. Native speakers have the same problem when they learn new language registers in their own cultures. Think of the difficulties you had in mastering the language and speaking style of your profession. In some professions, like medicine, the register is explicitly taught. For example, an important task for students in basic anatomy courses is to learn the technical names for every part of the anatomy; they usually do this while learning other things about bones, muscles, and so forth, so that they may not realise they are learning a language register. Some aspects of professional, business, and technical registers, however, are inevitably learned on the job, by listening to more experienced colleagues and hoping for the best. Because this is a hard task that can take years to accomplish, it is doubly hard to go into a new culture and discover that part but not all of the register is different. It is very frustrating to be de-skilled in this way, especially when the register has become so automatic in our native culture that it seems like 'plain talk'.

One feature of style and register that has received more attention in cross cultural research in recent years is the expression of politeness or *face* (see Brown & Levinson, 1978, 1987); we will take up this fascinating topic in more detail later. Face, which used to be thought of mainly as a phenomenon of Asian culture but which has in more recent times been shown to apply equally well in Western cultures, refers to communication that functions to enhance and maintain respect and esteem, as well as to avoid threatening the self-esteem of others. All of us know intuitively that life at work is an almost continuous exercise in face management and communication repair. We constantly misunderstand or are misunderstood, accidentally step on someone's toes (literally or metaphorically), overstep our own power, try to cover our backs after taking a risk, or cover up after an error. We also frequently have to give bad news, criticise, give orders, impose on others, and so forth—this is the nature of work under stress. We have a whole repertoire of communication at our command to smooth this process, but different languages and different dialect groups in the same language have different ways of doing this. Even sub-groups in the same dialect, such as members of different social classes or different genders, show fairly large differences in their ways of maintaining and repairing face. This goes far beyond what can be found in etiquette books, although these books were an early attempt to make conventions about politeness explicit for formal settings; with all their limitations, they were a worthwhile endeavour.

For the moment, a true story from our own organisation illustrates how subtle and tricky conventions about politeness can be to negotiate across cultures. A Dutch colleague, Paul, was visiting Australia for a fairly extended period and working in our organisation. He was a fluent English speaker, and a very friendly, gregarious, and charming person with a good deal to contribute, so he found himself in demand at presentations, meetings, and social events. He frequently got into trouble, however, because he said, as his Australian colleagues put it, 'exactly what he thinks, with no consideration for anybody's feelings'. What this meant is that when he did not want to do something, he simply said no, without explanation or apology; when he criticised another person, he told them exactly what he thought was wrong without preamble or qualification. He thought he was being helpful, and not beating around the bush; the Australians thought he was rude.

As things got more and more tense, a junior Australian member of the organisation, Jane, thought she had figured out what was going wrong—she was aware that in Dutch, more direct speech is preferred, while in Australian English, negative comments are couched in a great deal of qualification and softening. So she decided to talk to Paul and set him straight. Their conversation went approximately like this:

JANE: Paul, you know that Australians sometimes have rather bad stereotypes about Dutch people . . .

PAUL: Really? Why is that?

JANE: Well, Australians think Dutch people are rude because they always say exactly what they think—they don't soften anything down to take account of other people's feelings. You know, a Dutch worker on a building site or something might say, 'you put that scaffolding up badly', while we would say something like, 'perhaps you could think about strengthening up the scaffolding a bit'. It's amazing how rude and inconsiderate Aussies think Dutch people are as a result.

PAUL: That's absolutely fascinating—I wonder why they think that.

Here is a clear-cut case of communication at cross-purposes. Jane maintained the Australian polite style by criticising Paul in a very indirect and general way. When asked later why she did not speak more directly, she responded, 'I couldn't—it would have been too rude.' Paul, in his turn, did not recognise the point of the story at all. This left Jane frustrated and Paul none the wiser—and the stereotypes each held of the other's culture were only confirmed.

One of the most interesting features about misunderstandings that stem from cultural practices, conventions, or rules is that people from both cultures may see the problem as coming from a lack of competence in the language. Even in a case like the one above, there is often a tendency to conclude that the misunderstanding would not have occurred if only the other person were more fluent in the language. Here we see a good example of people jumping to the obvious, but not necessarily the correct, conclusion. If a foreigner or newcomer is very fluent in the language of the new culture, or is even a native speaker of a different dialect, the misunderstanding is more likely to have come from differences in some other aspect of communication. It is very tempting, however, to explain everything away in terms of language problems. As we will see in later chapters, this explanation leads to solutions that do not address the real problem.

## Misunderstandings Based in Cultural Values

People in every culture have a set of values by which they live. Some people can easily express these values, which may be tied to religious beliefs or ethical principles. For others, values are more a question of intuitions, the feeling that some kind of behaviour is right or wrong. While some values, perhaps the most important ones, appear to be universal across cultures (for example, all cultures have sanctions against murder, incest, and robbery), other values vary significantly. Probably the best-known example of this kind of difference has to do with the importance of the individual relative to the group. For most Western cultures, the individual (including individual rights and human rights) comes first. In many Asian and some Latin American cultures, however, the group comes first, so that the emphasis is on loyalty, promoting group harmony, and improving the lot of the greatest number of people. This basic difference in values has been called *individualism* versus *collectivism* (see Hofstede, 1980).

There are a number of other basic value dimensions on which cultures have been found to differ, including the acceptability of large power differentials, the importance of being certain about outcomes, and role differentiation between men and women. In addition, some aspects of the culture, such as preserving the group's language and the importance of the group's history, are more important in one culture than in another. Smolicz (1979) has described these important values as cultural core values. Often, as important as they are, they are not talked about; in some cases, there are even cultural taboos on talking about them. As a result, when people from two cultures interact, they may assume that they have the same values, whereas if they checked, they would discover that they do not.

It is fair at this point to ask what values have to do with communication. Is it not true that people's different values will surface eventually, and they will then have to use communication to negotiate some way to resolve their differences? The answer to this question is yes and no. When value differences or clashes come up, they do have to be negotiated, and in this sense they are independent of the way they are talked about. On the other hand, as we will discuss later, to some extent culture *is* communication, in that cultural knowledge, including values, are communicated constantly. For example, in cultures of British ethnicity, the emphasis on the individual appears all through the language, in proverbs ('every man for himself'; 'don't judge a book by its cover'), metaphors ('let's make sure we have a level playing field'), and communication practices that ensure equity and fairness, including a strong accent on explicit and clear instructions about any new task.

In business negotiations with people from collectivist cultures, this individualism can get in the way. For example, Japanese business people operating as collectives (*kiretsu*) can outbid American, Australian, or British companies, because they agree as a group on the price they want. In the case of coal pricing, for the past decade Australian companies have gone to the negotiating table with Japanese buyers as independent operators, competing against each other, and have therefore taken a lower price than they would have if they operated as a collective group.

One way we become aware that values are important is the discomfort we feel in a different culture when our own values seem to be trampled on. In many Western universities, for instance, foreign students from Asian countries are marked down on written work because they have incorporated long quotations from the published literature. Their professors feel quite justified in doing this, because the long quotations are evidence to the professors of lack of originality: there is 'nothing of the student's own work' in the essay. For their part, the students are unhappy about the situation, because they believe it is very important to show that they have read the work of earlier scholars, understand it, appreciate it, and respect it. Like their professors, they have learned this value in their home culture and communicated it to the best of their ability. When counsellors who are trying to help the students advise them to abandon this value and write in a more Western style, the students often say they are uncomfortable abandoning their respect for earlier scholars, as well as resentful that their professors seem to lack respect for their ideas and beliefs. Sometimes, they even see the professors' behaviour as racist. When this happens, neither the students nor the professors may be willing to examine their own values, or to ask themselves if there might not be another way of looking at what is good and bad in an essay.

## CULTURE SHOCK AND ADAPTATION

The anecdotes we have presented in this chapter all involve miscommunication or misunderstanding resulting from different language, style, rules, or values. It would be easy to think this is the whole story, and that if we could only have a dictionary that told us the rules and practices of each new culture we entered (something like a cultural version of the babel fish in Adams', 1980, *The Hitchhikers' Guide to the Galaxy*), we would have no problems in dealing with others. Whenever we conduct a workshop on intercultural communication, this is one of the major hopes of the participants—that somehow we can provide them with such a dictionary or book of rules. Unfortunately, there is more to it than that—even when they know the rules, people often misunderstand (deliberately or unintentionally) others from different cultures, or are frustratingly unsuccessful when they try to get work done.

One contributor to miscommunication that we have not yet discussed is culture shock (see Bochner, 1982, 1986). It may be exciting and challenging, but the simple fact of being in a strange environment is stressful and tiring. The simplest thing—catching a taxi, finding a room, getting food—is difficult. In addition, all the normal routines of life are disrupted, and nothing seems to work. Worse yet, none of the natives seems to have any understanding of how hard everything is. Just getting through the day can be a major effort, without having to cope with people who do things differently, and behave in sometimes inexplicable ways. The difficulty does eventually go away, but can last a surprisingly long time, especially if the traveller does not have a good command of the language in the host country.

Eventually, sojourners in a new culture start to adapt, if they stay long enough. This process brings its own challenges, which we will take up in more detail later. One problem for many medium- and long-term sojourners is how much to adapt, and how much of the old culture to give up. Take the case of Americans in Europe, or the analogous case of Europeans in Asian countries, working for large multinational organisations. Some of these people make great efforts to learn the language of the host country, and to become familiar with its customs and rules. In doing this, they begin to be cut off from their own compatriots: they are often described by other Americans as 'going native'. Sometimes, this has a detrimental effect on their work, and it nearly always leads to a feeling of either disloyalty to the old culture or resentment of other Americans for not adapting, or both. There is constant pressure on the accommodators from those Americans who do not adapt to come back into the fold: to have American friends, to read and watch American media, to act as if 'we are at home'. Meanwhile, people in the host country can be quite hostile to Americans who refuse to adapt—yet they do not always appreciate efforts to adapt either, as these people can threaten their sense of loyalty to their culture.

What happens to Americans in Europe happens to sojourners everywhere, if they stay long enough and have a large enough number of members of their old culture around them (see Kim, 1988). It seems as if, to adapt to the new culture, we have to give up the old one. We may be happy to give up the parts of the old culture we did not like in the first place, but when the values and practices that are important to us are challenged, it hurts to discard them.

In addition, our identity is bound up in many facets of our culture, and it can be surprising how hard it is to give these things up. For example, a British colleague of ours believed so strongly in being on time that he would leave people waiting on street corners or at his office door if they were even a few minutes late. To him, being late meant that the other person did not respect him and did not care about him (in fairness to him, he practised what he preached; he was never late for any appointment or date). His sense of his own identity was bound up in his ideas about promptness, and he was unable to give them up. You can imagine the trouble he had when he went to a culture where promptness was not valued at all. Differences in the value of time also exist not only within one culture but also across businesses with different organisational cultures. Even in the same city or industry, different organisational cultures lead to different values about time, dress, levels of formality, and ways of communicating.

Some people find they cannot meet the challenge of adaptation, and they either leave the culture or withdraw psychologically from it. We believe, however, that it is possible to become intercultural or multicultural; that is, to take on many characteristics of a new culture without losing the essential parts of one's own. An important part of doing this is clarifying our own core values; as it were, finding our personal bottom lines for behaviour and communication. Once we do this, it is much easier to have respect and tolerance for the practices of others, even if we do not like some practices and will not engage in them ourselves.

Another important part of the process is confronting our own prejudice towards the other culture, and our stereotypes about it. Usually, we do not want to admit to being prejudiced, and either deny that we are biased or find good rationalisations for our biases. In fact, a ubiquitous and quite normal aspect of social behaviour is the tendency to divide people into groups (*us* and *them*), and to find ways of distinguishing our own groups and making them look better than the outgroups (see Tajfel & Turner, 1979; Turner, 1987). It is virtually impossible *not* to be prejudiced, at least in some situations, as we will see in later chapters. It is possible, however, to have some understanding of how prejudice affects our communication, and to structure the situations we are in to minimise its influence.

## AIMS OF THE BOOK

As we said earlier, the main aim of this book is to apply the research of the last 50 years or so in cross-cultural psychology and related disciplines to making the task of intercultural communication easier and more effective. Part of this process is to give a perspective on culture that encourages open-mindedness and tolerance, but that also involves clarifying our own values and rules—finding our personal non-negotiable demands for interaction. In this way, we hope that the insights gained from this book will help to increase tolerance and reduce prejudice and discrimination among professional people who interact with those from other cultural, ethnic, and social groups. The bottom line is improved relationships and understanding within and across professional people and their organisations.

In later chapters, we will take up the research on social rules, to give a sense of the power and impact of these unseen contributors to our behaviour. We will look at the many ways cultures differ in their rules, and describe some strategies for navigating through this complex space. We will also examine the contributors to prejudice, especially including social identity and its impact on the self-concept and on stereotypes about people from our own groups and other groups. In doing this, we will try to give a sense of the variability in rules, identity, and even values within a culture. One of the major traps that travellers to other cultures fall into is thinking everyone from the new culture is the same, and, worse yet, treating them all as if they were the same. Finally, we will look at some specific contexts in the world of business and the professions where intercultural communication can be difficult, and once again describe some strategies for managing them.

Throughout the book, we will emphasise a number of principles. We set them out here as a first introduction, but we will return to them again and again. To us, they represent some points to keep in mind in any interaction, whether work or play, with a person from another culture or social group.

1. Respect loyalty to culture: people belong to cultures and feel loyalty to them, as they do to other important social groups.
2. Cultural bias is inevitable: cultures and other groups are sources of self-esteem, as well as knowledge, values, and beliefs.
3. Social rules influence communication: members of a culture share social rules which govern communication in many contexts.
4. Social rules are learned without being taught: they are also bound up with important values.
5. Cultural differences are not the only differences: people within a culture vary at least as much as people between cultures.

We hope you enjoy the book.

# 2

# VALUES AND RULES: THE IMPACT OF CULTURE ON COMMUNICATION

In Chapter 1, we presented some situations and features of culture that can lead to misunderstandings in intercultural encounters, and where such misunderstandings can contribute to negative stereotypes about people from another culture, and then to hostility, prejudice, discrimination, and ultimately conflict. As we noted there, misunderstanding is not the whole story; pre-existing prejudice, economic factors, and the history of relations between the cultures also play a role. Still, the many obvious and subtle ways in which cultures differ need to be understood and taken account of by any intercultural traveller, and in this chapter and the next one we explore them in some detail. Our aim is not to give a dictionary of these differences or a long list of cross-cultural examples and anecdotes, but to present some underlying principles which people can use in managing intercultural communication. If these principles are understood and followed, there is a good chance that cultural differences will be understood for what they are before they cause lasting damage to our social relationships. We aim to give the ounce of prevention that is worth a pound of cure.

This chapter deals with some of the values about which people in different cultures have different ideas, and goes on from there to explore the ways these values lead to social norms and rules about how we should behave in many situations. Then in Chapter 3 we take up language and the impact of culture not only on the language spoken but also on subtle language practices. Finally, we look at non-verbal behaviour—the voice and body movements that accompany speech, and which, while we are often not aware of them, are important channels for communicating who we are as individuals and as members of our cultures. Keep in mind that for many people the definition of culture is communication, as culture comprises the knowledge, beliefs, values, and practices that are constantly transmitted in conversation, written communication, and non-verbal behaviour.

## CULTURAL VALUES AND DIMENSIONS

As Robinson (1988) points out, a common trap into which those of us who work with people from other cultures often fall is to overemphasise the *similarities* between cultures. We believe that people are 'all the same under the skin', and that if we simply treat people politely and considerately as if they were members of our own culture, all will be well. Sometimes, this strategy works quite well, especially when the cultures involved are fairly near neighbours (e.g., two northern European cultures), when there is no special hostility between them to start off with, and when the encounter does not involve much conflict or sensitive negotiation. Such successful encounters may convince us that we can use this strategy in all intercultural encounters. Even when things go well, however, there are likely to have been small misunderstandings, which were easy to ignore in the overall pleasant and successful context. When things get tough, these misunderstandings may return to haunt us.

Of course, it is true that people in every culture confront the same basic life situations and challenges, so that there are some over-riding similarities in the ways in which we deal with them. We must all find ways to feed, clothe, and shelter ourselves, to reproduce and bring up the next generation, to deal with illness and death, to find relationships that sustain and protect us, and to find ways of expressing ourselves as individuals. There are some acts that threaten and hurt people in all cultures—thus, as we noted earlier, all cultures have strong sanctions against such acts as murder, robbery, rape, and incest. In addition, all cultures have deeply held values and norms about how power should be distributed, individual freedom, loyalty to the social group, how to deal with novel and ambiguous situations, and the ways in which roles in the culture should be divided up. In the case of social roles, this applies particularly to division of activities based on sex, which is the most basic and ubiquitous role dimension (followed closely by age) in all cultures.

Once we accept the universality of cultural features like those above, the differences start to surface. While cultures all confront individual freedom and loyalty to the group, for example, they do not all do it in the same way. For some cultures, the individual is paramount, whereas for others, the group takes precedence. Analogous differences exist for dealing with uncertainty, power, and role division. Research and training in cross-cultural communication has borrowed greatly from the work of Hofstede (1980, 1983), who explored the values of students, managers, and others in over 40 cultures. In the next sections, we present his four dimensions and examine briefly their impact on communication.

## Individualism–Collectivism

Resolving the tension between individual freedom and the welfare of the whole group is a challenge that has exercised all cultures for the whole history of civilisation. Many philosophers, both Eastern and Western, have explored this tension, and tried to find a balance between protecting the individual and protecting the group. Not surprisingly, a large number of balance points have resulted, and Hofstede (1980) found cultures across the whole range from extreme individualism (e.g., European Americans in the USA) to extreme collectivism (e.g., China). For many trainers in cross-cultural and intercultural communication, individualism–collectivism is the most important value dimension on which cultures can be compared. Certainly, the role of the individual versus the group causes disagreements between members of different cultures at every level from the large-scale political—consider the debates between countries about the importance of political freedom, for example—to the small-scale individual. Remember, though, that even the most extreme cultures on this dimension recognise the importance of both the individual and the group. In addition, most cultures are neither extremely individualist nor extremely collectivist, but fall somewhere in the middle. Finally, many countries are culturally very complex, and cannot be characterised simply as either collectivist or individualist. For example, European Americans in the USA are in the main very individualistic, while African Americans are less so, and the cultures of Latin Americans are on the collectivist side of this dimension.

For members of extreme individualist cultures like European Americans in the USA, individual rights and obligations come first. There is a strong emphasis on individual merit and competition, which is communicated in proverbs ('the early bird gets the worm') and words of wisdom (for example, Emerson's call to 'trust thyself' in his 'Essay on self reliance', (Ziff, 1982)). Individual rights are enshrined in law like the Bill of Rights in the US Constitution, protected by the adversarial system in the courts, which is shared with other Anglo-Saxon countries, and incorporated into elaborate procedures to ensure fairness in examinations at school, hiring for jobs, and the like (the well-known 'level playing field'). Individualism is expressed in values about the importance of doing your best, reward for individual achievement and the chance for success: as an American friend used to say, 'If you love your mother and work hard, there's always room at the top', and the importance of solving problems yourself, not waiting for others to do it for you.

One feature of individualism which can make intercultural interactions easier, if it is understood and used well, is a softness and permeability in the boundaries of group membership (Gallois et al., 1995; Tajfel & Turner, 1979). The individual is so important, it is relatively easy to forget the group from which the person came. Thus, it is common for European Americans to say sincerely, 'I treat everyone the same—it doesn't matter who it is, good work is rewarded and bad work is punished.' This ideal is not always met, but the fact that it exists can make members of individualist cultures more tolerant of outsiders. For example, an American colleague, visiting China for his company, was shocked and hurt when some Chinese people refused to speak to him (in fact, acted as if he were not in the room at all), because they had not been properly introduced. He said this would never happen at home, where individuals are always recognised. In collectivist cultures, the distinction between the ingroup and outgroup is much sharper, and outsiders may not be treated with the same consideration as insiders, which can be hard to handle for individualists.

The cost of individualism is paid in alienation from the group. In more collectivist cultures, the individual is given security by the group, whether it is the security of employment in a life-long job (as has been traditional in Japan, for example, or indeed some large Western corporations like IBM), or the guarantee of help and protection of the family (as in Italy, where pulling strings in the public sphere for family members is a well-accepted and much-used practice). Just as in individualist cultures, the obligations of individuals to the group, and of the group to them, are enshrined in the legal system and other social institutions, as well as in individual interactions. People from collectivist cultures often find it hard to deal with the open conflict, competitiveness, and aggressiveness of European Americans, because they have a much stronger value of maintaining harmony and good relations in the group. For them, rewards may come with seniority and age, rather than individual achievement. For example, Koreans go to a lot of trouble to discover who is older in a social interaction; the younger person (even if younger only by a few days or a year) is expected to defer to the elder, in the interests of harmony.

Sometimes, the concept of the 'level playing field' can cause problems in intercultural communication. Many of our colleagues in Australia (a culture which Hofstede classified with the USA and the UK as very individualistic), for example, believe that university examinations should be scrupulously fair, with all students working under exactly the same conditions. In this way, they believe, individual merit will shine through, and the students who have mastered the course material best will perform best. Thus, they are very reluctant to allow extra time for foreign students who have some problems with their written English—a common situation among foreign students everywhere, as written expression is usually the part of language that is performed least well by nonnatives. To them, this would not be 'fair' to the native students. Our colleagues have a hard time recognising that lack of fluency in English also results in a lack of fairness. In recent years, many Australian universities have stepped in with institutional rules about exam conditions for foreigners; they see a need to counteract these cultural norms in order to encourage overseas students to enrol in their courses. On the other hand, a professor in a more collectivist culture, who subscribes to a norm of helping the whole class to perform well, would probably have no qualms about providing extra time, once the foreign students were accepted into the class in the first place.

At the individual level, individualism and collectivism tend to produce different kinds of self-concept (Markus & Kitayama, 1991, 1994). People from individualist cultures are likely to have *independent* self-concepts, reflecting the culture in their sense of separateness from others. Those from more collectivist cultures, on the other hand, are likely to reflect their cultures in an *interdependent* self-concept, in which their sense of self is tied up with their relations to their group (family, work group, class at school). One result of the type of self-concept, according to Markus & Kitayama, is that people from individualist cultures tend to express emotion more freely than people from collectivist cultures, particularly for outwardly directed emotions like anger and contempt (see Scherer, 1988). Later, we will examine in more detail the ways in which individualism and collectivism affect other aspects of language and non-verbal communication.

Before leaving this dimension, one important point must be mentioned: cultures are not static in their values about individualism–collectivism, and not everyone in a culture has the same, or anything like the same, kind of self-concept with respect to it. In fact, some people in individualist cultures reject this social value (or appear to) and declare themselves to be collectivists; the same thing happens in reverse in collectivist cultures. Often these people are young adults, at a point in their lives where they are challenging the values of their own society. Thus, students (and managers) in Australia have been found in several studies to be just as collectivist as those in Hong Kong (Bochner, 1994)—or, alternatively, students in Hong Kong are just as individualist as Australians. Other studies have found that Australians (but not European Americans in the USA) are as collectivist as Japanese, but nevertheless are more individualist, which suggests that it is possible to hold collectivist and individualist values at the same time (Kashima et al., 1995).

What these studies may all be telling us, however, is that people within cultures are different and, depending on who you ask, one culture may look more individualistic or more collectivistic (Gudykunst et al., 1996; Singelis & Brown, 1995). In dealing with people from other cultures, then, we need to be ready for some surprises and not assume that every Chinese we come across will have a collectivist orientation and an interdependent self-concept, while every English person will be a strong individualist. What we can predict about these people, however, is that they will know the values and norms of their own culture about this dimension. This issue will be discussed further in later sections.

## Power Distance

Think about how you react to the power of other people, as well as how you expect your own subordinates to treat you. Do you expect more powerful people to be deferred to simply because they hold the positions they do, or do you expect everyone's ideas to be tested, and people to treat each other more or less as equals? Probably, your expectations are somewhere in-between these two extremes of power distance. Once again, cultures differ in how they think about the perquisites of power, particularly *legitimate power* (French & Raven, 1959), or power based on the position a person holds in a hierarchy. People in cultures with a high power distance (Hofstede, 1980) believe that more powerful people must be deferred to and not argued with, especially in public. Their status (based on age, seniority, or position) gives them the right to tell others what to do; indeed, in work contexts, their subordinates assume that they will be told what to do by these people. For members of cultures with low power distance, on the other hand, ideas are assumed to be equal, and people are expected to defend their ideas even against less powerful people. This leads to more deference being given to power based on knowledge and expertise, rather than status or position alone.

In intercultural interactions between people from cultures that differ in the preferred power distance, misunderstandings are plentiful. For example, O'Sullivan (1994) recounts the story of an employee given an assignment by his boss. The employee, from a high power-distance culture (like Greece or Japan) expected to be told what to do, and then to do it to the best of his ability. The supervisor, from a low power-distance culture (like the USA or Sweden) expected the employee, who was after all going to be the one to do the work, to take the initiative and negotiate how the job would be done. After several conversations, the boss described the subordinate as lacking in initiative and probably competence, while the subordinate described the supervisor as temperamental and indecisive.

In Western cultures, in addition, people are more relaxed about issues of status in social or public situations. Engholm (1991) notes that fist fights are common in Korea, as strangers meeting for the first time differ in their perceptions of who has the higher status. While many Asian cultures show a concern about where a stranger fits into the group, Westerners tend to be more focused on discussing the distinctive personality characteristics of the stranger as an individual, outside of any group membership.

Sometimes even subtle differences in power distance can lead to difficulties. Americans going to the United Kingdom or Australia to work, for example, often complain of the over-hierarchical system and of being stifled by having to 'toe the line' all the time. These cultures, all Anglo-Celtic in ethnic background, are close in power distance according to Hofstede's (1980) classification (that is, compared to other cultures), but they are still far enough apart that travellers notice the difference, and often become frustrated by it.

How do high power-distance cultures find ways to allow good ideas to come up from the bottom? Often, they do this by taking ideas out of the public sphere. Many companies and organisations in Japan, for instance, have procedures for making suggestions and developing ideas away from the public glare, sometimes even anonymously—perhaps not a palatable method for an extreme individualist. Then when the idea is presented publicly, the person with the highest status does the presenting on behalf of the whole group. On the other hand, low power-distance cultures also find ways of reinforcing the status of people who are higher in the hierarchy, from giving them bigger and better offices (Sommer, 1969) to developing communication norms that allow them to dominate (see below). In this case, the rewards of status are still there, but the realm of ideas can exist in a state of equality (or apparent equality anyway). Notice that in the examples given in this paragraph, high power distance is associated with collectivism, and low power distance with individualism; this is frequently but not always the case. For the intercultural traveller, the trick is to know the ways in which ideas are transmitted, and in which status and power are expressed, in the particular context.

## Uncertainty Avoidance

A third dimension of cultural difference concerns the extent to which uncertainty and ambiguity are tolerated. We all have a limit of uncertainty beyond which we feel uncomfortable; in fact, strangers in conversation use a number of strategies, including asking questions, disclosing information about the self, and trying to find common knowledge and experiences with the other person, that help to reduce uncertainty (see Berger & Bradac, 1982; Gudykunst, 1995). Nevertheless, some cultures tolerate very little ambiguity and uncertainty in interactions, relative to others. People in these cultures want to 'know where they stand', and they have rituals, forms of address, and uncertainty-reducing strategies to help them in this. It may be very appropriate in these cultures, for example, to state your occupation and company, the place where you live, and even your age and salary, upon first being introduced. For instance, in Japan it is quite common to say the name of your company before your own name when you introduce yourself. Indeed, members of these cultures may take considerable risks (even to the point of starting fights) in order to reduce uncertainty. For members of cultures where more uncertainty is tolerated, on the other hand, other values (privacy, modesty, even excitement) have more importance, and strangers are kept guessing about each other for a longer period.

Perhaps it is no surprise that high uncertainty avoidance tends to go with collectivism and high power distance, while tolerance of uncertainty goes with individualism and lower power distance. There are, of course, some interesting exceptions, like individualist France, where uncertainty avoidance is high. These three dimensions often combine into a package where strangers from outside the group are welcomed, and their 'unusual' behaviour is tolerated and even a source of fascination. In more collectivist cultures, the addition of high power distance and uncertainty avoidance helps to sharpen the insider–outsider distinctions. In these cultures, it can take a long time to get in; for example, it is estimated that only one in 25 Japanese–American business negotiations will lead further. Once you are in, though, you are really in, and people may discuss the most personal details of their lives with you (see Engholm, 1991). The amount of disclosure and intimacy that are expressed can be disconcerting to people from individualist cultures, who are used to a more tolerant, but in the end less intimate, relationship with a large number of people. Overall, we must learn to do business and to manage interactions on other people's terms.

## Masculinity–Femininity

Hofstede (1980) named this dimension to capture the ways in which cultures differ in the sharpness of their sex-role distinctions, and more generally, in the extent to which people in the culture behave in similar ways. The name he gave to this dimension is not the happiest of choices, as sex roles are only part of it. Nevertheless, cultures higher in masculinity do tend to have sharp distinctions in the behaviour expected of men and women, while high-feminine cultures (like the

Scandinavian countries) have strong norms and values promoting equality between the sexes. Interestingly enough, this dimension is probably the least associated with individualism–collectivism. For example, Anglo-Saxon cultures, which are fairly extreme on individualism, low power distance, and tolerance of uncertainty, fall in the middle of the masculinity–femininity dimension.

Cultural differences in the ways in which sex roles and family roles are expressed often form a very sensitive area, especially for Westerners, whose ideas about sex and gender are in a state of fairly rapid change. It can be very difficult for Western people, particularly women from Anglo-Saxon cultures, who have only fairly recently accepted the idea of equality between the sexes, to deal with a Malaysian colleague's wife who greets them for dinner but then does not take any part in the conversation. It can be just as hard to cope with criticism from the other side—for example, with a Swedish colleague who is vociferous in his condemnation of 'cruelty to children', by which he means spanking at home and corporal punishment at school, in England.

## CULTURE AND SOCIAL RULES

After the Second World War, many Americans began to travel abroad for business, in the army, and in the diplomatic service. They soon noticed that they were receiving a less-than-enthusiastic welcome. This was the era of 'the ugly American', when people from the USA seemed to violate every norm and custom in every country they visited. They were stereotyped as aggressive and uncultured interlopers. Needless to say, this caused great anxiety among the travellers, and was one of the major sources of the training programmes in cross-cultural and intercultural communication that exist today.

Much of what we do today in intercultural communication we owe to the pioneering work of E.T. Hall (1959, 1966, 1976),

who spent many years doing research and developing training programmes for the US diplomatic service. Hall did not
talk about rules as such, but described several types of communication codes, which are linked to cultural values and
which govern our behaviour in many situations. His concept
of codes is very similar to the concept of social rules developed by Argyle and his colleagues in England (Argyle,
Furnham & Graham, 1981; Argyle & Henderson, 1985). They
define *social rules* something like this: *shared expectations about
the behaviour that should and should not occur in specific social
situations.*

Like Hall's codes, rules according to this definition are shared
by some or most people in a society, rather than private to one
or a few individuals. In addition, they are normative; that is,
they are backed by moral principles or notions of right and
wrong. Rules are expectations; that is, they may not actually
be followed in real behaviour, but people think they will be.
Finally, they are specific to particular situations, although
Argyle and his colleagues have found a small number of rules
that seem to apply in many situations.

Here are some examples of rules in Western cultures, taken
from a number of sources (e.g., Argyle, Furnham & Graham,
1981; Argyle & Henderson, 1985; Grice, 1975; Hall, 1959, 1966;
Wilson & Gallois, 1993). Check them against your ideas about
how to behave in different situations. Do they ring true? Are
they generally followed? What happens when they are
violated?

1. Treat other people with respect—don't make them feel
   small.
2. When you talk to others, look them in the eye to show
   respect.
3. Arrive for appointments at the time arranged, or no more
   than a minute or two afterwards.
4. Arrive at dinner parties between 10 and 30 minutes after
   the time arranged.

5. When you speak, be brief and to the point.
6. When you refuse a request, give an explanation for why you can't do what the other person is asking.
7. Defend yourself against unfair criticism from superiors, colleagues, and subordinates.
8. When you converse with another person, stand between ½ and 1 metre away from them.

Interestingly enough, all these rules, with the possible exception of the first one (one of Argyle, Furnham & Graham's, 1981, universal rules) are culture-bound. Thus, there are many cultures that either do not have these rules or, more likely, have different rules covering the same type of behaviour. A few examples will illustrate what we mean.

> *Example 1.* In the USA, a European American manager calls in his African American subordinate to give him some instructions. While he is talking, the subordinate stares at the floor. This makes the manager angry, as he sees it as a sign of disrespect, so he speaks aggressively to the subordinate. The subordinate then looks at him, but when he leaves the office, he complains to senior management that his supervisor is unfair and racist, which does the manager no good at all.

What has happened here? Essentially, the manager subscribes to the rule that you should look other people in the eye when they are talking to you. The subordinate, however, is following the African American rule that respect is shown by looking away from the other person. Many other cultures share this rule, by the way—looking people in the eye is a sign of challenge and disrespect. When the manager gets what he wanted, it is in fact because the subordinate is angry and has lost respect for him, but he is unaware of this until the complaint arrives.

> *Example 2.* An American working in Germany is invited to the home of one of her colleagues for dinner at 8 pm on a Friday. She arrives at about 8:20. The German host greets

her at the door, but seems a bit cold and angry. They sit down to dinner almost immediately; as they eat, the room thaws out a bit, but it takes most of the evening for things to come really right.

This time, the American has not been prompt enough; Germans follow a rule that says you should be on time, or even a little early, for all appointments. If the shoe had been on the other foot and the Germans had been coming to her house, she may have been put out by their over-prompt arrival, but as things stand, they are put out by what they see as her tardiness. Notice that no one says anything about any of this; it just causes some frost in the atmosphere. Interestingly enough, the American (let alone the Germans) may have been similarly annoyed by Latin American colleagues, who follow a rule that says you should be up to an hour or more late for appointments of this kind.

> *Example 3.* A Japanese manager is visiting Australia on business. He asks an Australian colleague to explain a new procedure to him. The Australian tells him quickly, precisely, and from scratch, how the procedure works, points to a couple of possible problems, and asks him if he has any questions. The manager feels that he has been treated like a child, and that the Australian has no consideration for his feelings.

In this case, the Australian has followed the rule that you should be brief and to the point when you speak. He has also not made any assumptions about what the Japanese manager knows already, but has explained everything briefly and succinctly. What he has not done is to follow the Japanese rule that you should find common ground with other people when explaining things to them, and work from what they know. He has also violated the rule, which the Japanese manager subscribes to, that you should build a good relationship before going on to do a work task. All this leaves the Japanese feeling insulted, while the Australian may not be aware of the problem at all.

These examples have a lot in common, and as a group they illustrate a number of features of rules. First, as Hall (1959) pointed out very cogently, rules are *unspoken*; they are often learned without being taught, and there may even be taboos about discussing them. This means that rules are *automatic*; they seem like the 'natural, obvious thing to do' to people who follow them, who may not even be aware they have a rule until someone breaks it. When the rule is broken by one person, even when that person is from another country and is a new visitor or a tourist, the other person immediately jumps to the conclusion that the rule violator did it deliberately and knowingly. Thus, rules have *moral force*, and are tied to important cultural values like those we described above. When a rule is broken, we tend to conclude that the person who did it had the same motivation we would have had if we had done it. For example, if a man stands too close to a woman, he must be making a sexual advance; if he stands too far away, he must not like or respect her. But how close is too close? How far is too far?

Some rules are more important than others, in the sense that they are more closely tied to cultural core values. Hall (1959) called these *formal codes*, and he noted that they are usually learned by punishment—little reward for doing the right thing, and little explanation, but punishment for 'being a bad boy or girl' for violating them. This means it can be almost impossible to distinguish the behaviour, the rule, the value it is tied to, and our emotional reaction of outrage and anger at a violation.

Rules about how far to stand from another person, and how to orient towards them when speaking to them (e.g., face-on for Arabs; at a 45 degree angle for Anglo-Saxons; side-to-side for Chinese), fall into this category in most cultures. This is because rules about where to stand are linked to values about sexuality, aggression, and respect—the 'right' distance is morally right. The 'right' distance, of course, varies with the personal relationship; we can stand closer to intimate friends, family members, children, and animals than we can to strangers or colleagues. Unfortunately, all of these rules exist well below the surface of awareness for most people, so that when they are broken, we are aware of the moral violation ('he treated me really aggressively and with no respect at all') but not always of the behaviour that caused it (he stood too close). Even when we are aware of the behaviour, we may describe it in morally loaded words: 'he was all over me like a rash', meaning he was standing too close and perhaps he touched me, which violated another of my culture's rules.

## Rules, Relationships, and Context

Not only are most rules culture-bound, they are also context-bound; as the definition above states, rules are *specific to situations*. In addition, they are often specific to roles. For example, one study found that Australians believe it is appropriate for employees to discuss their personal limitations with their supervisors, but it is inappropriate for supervisors to do so with their employees (Bryan & Gallois, 1992). In another example, some women in the USA feel that it is appropriate and expected for them to express all their emotions, but men must keep their emotions under control (see Lutz, 1990).

The complication increases because cultures are different not only in the rules they apply in a situation, but also in the people and roles they apply them to. For example, in many Middle Eastern and some Asian cultures, it is appropriate for same-sex people to walk hand-in-hand in the street, but not for opposite-sex people to do so. In Western cultures, this rule is applied the other way around. Thus, we cannot assume, once we think we have learned a rule in another culture, that we know its scope—who it applies to, where, and when.

## Dealing with Cultural Rule Differences

As a way of preventing misunderstandings based on rule differences like these, Hall (1959, 1966, 1976) recommends bringing the rules to the surface and becoming more aware of them. There is much to be said for this strategy. The first step in it is to become more aware of your own rules about behaviour, at least for situations where you are likely to meet people from other cultures or sub-cultures. Many years ago, Rom Harré (see Harré & Secord, 1972) devised a fascinating but risky way of doing this. He deliberately violated what he believed were rules for public behaviour (for example, he was impolite to the hostess at parties), then observed what happened and how long it took other people to repair the situation. His logic was that the more important the rule, the longer it would take and the harder it would be to repair the situation. Eventually, of course, his friends and colleagues got used to it, and when he broke a rule, their reaction was, 'Oh, that's just Rom Harré doing another experiment.' Even so, he learned a lot about social rules in the process.

Most of us are not in a position to imitate this method, if only because we do not wish to risk our social relationships. Nevertheless, we can use it to do thought experiments. Imagine what it would be like if you belched all the way through dinner; addressed your family with title and last name ('Mr Smith', 'Miss Jones'); sat on the chair arm of a colleague while you conversed; showed up 15 minutes late for a work appointment; gave a job to your subordinate without explaining what he should do. What would the reaction be? What would other people conclude about your motives and intentions, and why? How long would it take to repair the situation? What would be the consequences for your relationship? Such experiments can give us a lot of insight into our own social rules.

It is probably impossible to become conscious of all our own social rules, and certainly impossible to learn all those of other cultures, no matter how hard we try. The dream of a cross-cultural 'rule dictionary' must remain in the realms of fantasy. The thought experiments we described above, however, can go a long way towards preventing misunderstandings based on rule differences, because they *break the nexus between behaviour and interpretations of it*. If we can slow ourselves down enough, we can become aware of behaviour that violates a rule *before* we conclude that the other person had a malicious reason for doing it, and we can imagine that the other person might be following a different rule. In other words, we can give the other person the benefit of the doubt. Similarly, if we get the impression that we have upset another person, we can imagine that we may have violated a rule of theirs, and we can ask them about it; even if they refuse to discuss it, the anger in the situation can be defused in this way.

It must be said that in some cases, this is easier said than done. Some years ago, one of us was visiting a large city with a multicultural population, and riding a tram. The tram was fairly crowded, and I was standing, holding onto a strap with one hand, and holding the newspaper I was reading with the other (following Anglo-Celtic rules and conventions for tram-riding). Suddenly, I noticed that someone behind me was tapping me repeatedly on the back. I stiffened in horror— what could this mean? Then I realised that the person behind me was talking to another person in Greek. I thought, 'You're an expert in cross-cultural differences in communication; you can handle this.' I remembered that Greeks have different rules for handling crowding, and I imagined that the other person might be treating me as a non-person—perhaps using me as a kind of wall to gesture on. This made me feel proud of my expertise, but I was still very uncomfortable about being tapped again and again. So I stood in stiff silence through the rest of the ride.

In hindsight, I could have handled the situation better, by politely moving away from the people or by politely telling them I preferred that they didn't tap on my back. This would have made me feel better, and might have made them more aware of differences from their own rules. In many cases, though, rules are so well-learned and so grounded in our emotional reaction that knowledge is not enough to stop the gut reaction to violations. My knowledge about social rules, however, did slow me down enough that I did not immediately take the behaviour personally, or draw negative conclusions about these people in particular or Greeks in general. That may be enough to rescue many potentially destructive situations.

## Values, Rules, and Tolerance: Finding Your Own Cultural Bottom Line

Throughout this chapter, we have pointed to the need to be open-minded about cultural differences in values and rules. The first step in this process is to become aware that cultures *are* different, even though people in them may have many common characteristics, goals, and problems. As long as we think our values and rules are natural, moral, and the only way to deal with a situation, our communication with people from other cultures will be far less effective. It is important to keep in mind that cultures derive their values for good reasons, even if they are different from our own. For example, an American individualist may have a hard time understanding the reluctance of Chinese colleagues to stand out from the crowd, and their insistence on agreeing on everything in advance. Even so, the American should be able to recognise the importance of maintaining good group relationships, which is what motivates this behaviour. Brislin and Yoshida (1994) call this process becoming *ethnorelative*: recognising that our ways are not the only ways to do things; there are other ways that are usually based on values and principles that are just as important as our own.

Next, we need to take account of the fact that many values and rules are unspoken; people may not even be aware of them until they are violated in some way. We need to slow down our own reactions long enough to be aware of the behaviour that caused them before we draw conclusions about what the other person meant by the behaviour. Similarly, if a person from another culture reacts in a surprising way, we need to imagine that we may have unknowingly violated one of that person's rules. Then, it is important to give the other person the benefit of the doubt—to assume that the person was well motivated, but was following a different set of rules. If there is any doubt about this, we can check it out. Most of the time, it turns out that the other person did have a different rule. Thus, misunderstanding is reduced, and our and that person's stock of good cross-cultural anecdotes is increased. In the small number of cases where it turns out that the person's behaviour was intended to hurt us, at least we know we haven't drawn any unwarranted conclusions.

It should be noted that there are some cases where people in another culture violate a value that is so important to us that we cannot go along with them. For example, if we believe in equality between the sexes, we may not be able to tolerate the restrictions placed on women in some highly masculine cultures. Similarly, if we believe in promoting the welfare of the group, we may disapprove strongly of cut-throat competition and the dishonest behaviour that sometimes goes along with it. Cultivating an open mind and a sense of ethnorelativity does not mean thinking that all values are equally right. We are aware of this in our own culture, and the same thing applies when we interact with people from another culture.

How we handle situations where important values of ours really are being violated is a difficult moral question, and we cannot hope to answer it in this book. We can say that there may be times when we must end a relationship, leave a culture, or take action against another person. Fortunately, for the majority of intercultural interactions, this does not happen; such crucially important values are not really involved. Rather, rules and sometimes values are different, but it is possible to understand where people in the other culture are coming from, even if we would do things differently. Needless to say, it is essential to be able to distinguish situations where important values are really at issue from situations where rule differences are involved, if we are to communicate successfully with people from other cultures. Thus, we must learn what our own cultural bottom line is—the values where we can negotiate, but we cannot compromise. The rest of the time, we can allow others to be different, and respect their differences as they respect ours.

In summary, we can follow a series of steps in finding our way through the maze of social rules and values in our own and other cultures:

1. Be aware that cultures are different in the balance they strike for many important values—especially individualism versus collectivism, high versus low power distance, high versus low uncertainty avoidance, and masculinity versus femininity.
2. Be aware that social rules are expectations derived from values, and have normative force; they too differ from one culture to another.
3. Become aware of our own values and rules, by imagining what it would be like if they were violated.
4. Develop an open mind about the motives, values, and rules behind other people's behaviour. Cultivate respect for other rules in cultures where things are done differently.
5. Become aware of our own cultural bottom lines. Learn to distinguish really important values that cannot be compromised from culturally based preferences about how to do things.

In the next chapter, we will deal with some specific consequences of values and rules for language and non-verbal behaviour.

# 3

# CULTURE, LANGUAGE, AND NON-VERBAL COMMUNICATION

When we interact with people from other cultures, it helps to speak the same language, literally and metaphorically. As we will see, this is not always an easy task, because much of the time, there are few exact translations from one culture to another. In the previous chapter, cultural values were examined, and we explored the ways in which they determine many of the important rules we subscribe to. In this chapter, we will look in some detail at the micro-level features of communication, in order to describe some of the most important differences and dimensions of communication. Once again, we will not attempt to follow the approach of a cross-cultural dictionary, as this is an impossible task—even bilingual dictionaries leave a lot out, and they only deal with the meanings of individual words. Instead, we will continue to emphasise strategies that can be used to prevent misunderstandings, to pick them up as soon as they occur, or to minimise their negative consequences for good relationships and for getting the task done.

## LANGUAGE: THE MEDIUM OF INFORMATION

The words that make up language are ideal for expressing ideas, thoughts, and beliefs, as well as conveying information.

Their linear structure and the strict rules they follow are well-suited to getting across explicit information, as a given word only has a small number of possible meanings, and words can be arranged in only a small number of different orders to mean different things. In most cultures, language is used when people want to get ideas and information across efficiently, although they are not always successful in accomplishing this task. In addition, people use language when they wish to own or take responsibility for the information. Because it is explicit and follows strict rules, language is relatively easy to remember.

Just as they differ about values and rules, cultures differ in their approach to the use of language, even though all cultures rely on language as the major way of getting information across to others. In fact, the structure and use of language is closely tied to cultural values. Language is an excellent medium for transmitting these values, as the next section shows.

## Cultural Values and Language: High-context and Low-context Language

Cultural values are a basic part of the communication agenda. Values affect the way language is used to ensure equity or to enhance group harmony. Individualist cultures tend to use what Hall (1976, 1995; also see Gudykunst, 1991) calls *low-context* language. Low-context language assumes no inside knowledge on the part of the listener. In principle, everything is explained. It involves step-by-step explanations, arranged in some logical order (for example, chronological order), without extraneous information, but with everything a person could need to follow it. Ideally, the language is so clear that a complete stranger to the culture and the situation can understand it. Here is an example of low-context language, in which a supervisor gives instructions to an employee:

This report is for Mr Smith, the Director of Personnel Services. He needs to know the way we went about hiring the
last group of management trainees, because he'll pass it on
to other sections for them to use in their selection process.
You should start the report by listing the selection criteria
for the training programme, then go on to the way we
recruited applicants from inside and outside the company—
our use of personal letters to potential applicants, the electronic bulletin boards, and so forth—then the procedures
we used to select the people who interviewed applicants,
and the way we selected the trainees after the interviews.
It's best to present the procedures in chronological order.
Make the report brief—5 pages or less—and it's fine to use
bullet points for the most important information. You need
to address the report to Mr Smith, but include copies for Mr
Jones and Ms Wilson, the CEO, too, as well as all the members of the interview panel. Is that clear? Do you have any
questions about the report, or do you need any more detail?

As you can see, this language contains a good bit of repetition
and redundancy. It is explicit enough that a person who is not
familiar with the company's selection process can understand
it easily.

Collectivistic cultures, on the other hand, show their desire to
maintain harmony and good relations within the group, as
well as sharp boundaries between insiders and outsiders, by
the *high-context* quality of their language. High-context language assumes inside knowledge on the part of the listener,
and takes advantage of this knowledge by leaving many details out of the explanation. Instead, more effort is put into
maintaining a good relationship between the speaker and the
listener, and on promoting the group generally. A high-
context version of the instructions above might look something like this:

I know you will do a good job with this report—you are so
familiar with the trainees and the programme. Mr Smith
will be very pleased. He said he wants to know everything

we did, from start to finish. Don't go into too much detail, though—you know how tiring it is to read endless reports. Mr Jones and Ms Wilson are keen to see it too—everyone is. I'm really pleased with our trainees and the way we selected them—we have a procedure other sections should follow, don't you think? Thanks very much for doing such a great job with it.

This paragraph, at first glance, does not look to be long and strong on information—it would not be possible to do the report without prior familiarity with the job selection process, as well as the roles of people in the company. These high-context instructions hint at things ('you know how tiring it is to read endless reports') that the earlier instructions made explicit ('make the report brief—5 pages or less'), as well as giving no detail about the contents or the structure of the report. What the high-context instructions do contain, however, is information about relationships ('I know you will do a good job'; 'Mr Smith will be very pleased'; I'm really pleased with our trainees'; 'thanks for doing such a great job'). In fact, the high-context paragraph also reveals what the low-context instructions left out—there is nothing in the low-context instructions about the confidence of the supervisor in the person writing the report, or the success of the programme. In addition, the strong hints about organisational politics in the high-context instructions would be easy to overlook in the low-context ones. In other words, the supervisor using high-context instructions is making maximum use of the inside knowledge of the listener, and the 'cryptic' paragraph turns out to contain a great deal of information—for those who can understand it.

Notice that neither paragraph contains absolutely everything needed to write the report—even the supervisor using low-context language has to assume some knowledge on the part of the employee. It is a matter of degree, and of where the emphasis is put: on making the task clear and easy to follow, or on stressing the importance of the relationship and the group. In low-context languages, good relationships and good motivation on the part of individual speakers tend to be assumed, which is sometimes frustrating even for members of individualistic cultures who can feel that they never get any positive feedback for their work. In high-context language, relationships and group harmony are constantly reinforced, but knowledge about how to do the task may be assumed. This makes things difficult for beginners and strangers, who must be patient and feel their way to the correct procedures for doing the job.

The use of high-context or low-context language is without doubt one of the most challenging and frustrating aspects of communication between people in individualistic and collectivistic cultures (see Gudykunst, 1991). As is the case with so many important social rules, rules about the explicitness of language are learned without being taught, so that people tend to think that their language has 'got it right' in some absolute sense, or that theirs is the only way to communicate clearly and effectively. When they are confronted with someone who leaves out what they consider to be important information, Westerners from individualistic cultures can feel as though they are deliberately being kept in the dark about the job. They may go on to conclude that the other person is trying to make them fail, or is withholding information for personal gain, or is just 'being inscrutable'. Of course, in some cases this may be true; high-context language can be an excellent strategy for keeping competitors guessing during bargaining and negotiation, for instance. On the other hand, it is also simply the way people who speak high-context languages talk.

Like their Western counterparts, speakers from collectivistic cultures who use high-context languages, when they are confronted with a low-context speaker, often feel insulted, for two main reasons. First, the other person insists on giving them a lot of information they feel they don't need—after all, they may understand the detail of the situation even better than the other person. Secondly, there is often little in low-context language to reinforce the relationship or praise the listener, so that people from collectivistic cultures may feel that the other person doesn't care about them—the only important thing is getting the job done, and they are being exploited. Of course, this also may be true; individualistic cultures often value getting things done quickly ('time is money'), and it may be in a person's individual interest to use others to get results. On the other hand, this is also simply the way people who speak low-context languages talk.

When we think of high-context and low-context languages, just as when we think of collectivistic and individualistic cultures, the obvious examples that come immediately to mind are Chinese and Japanese on the high-context side, and English and French on the low-context side. In fact, though, there is a range on this dimension too. For example, English and French are indeed low-context languages, compared to Chinese and Japanese—but German is even lower context. E.T. Hall (1995) presents a salutary example, which shows that even speakers of low-context languages can be 'low contexted'.

The example concerns a French manager employed by a German company. Most of the other people in the company were Germans, and the Frenchman already felt a little isolated as a result. On top of this, he felt he was constantly being insulted by his colleagues, who seemed to treat him like a child. For instance, when they gave him directions, they would say something like, 'Leave the building by the front door, and turn left. Walk up to the corner and cross the street—make sure the light is green!—then count five doors until you come to number 28. Turn left into that building, find the lifts in front of you, and go to the fifth floor—the reception desk is right in front of you.' This kind of thing happened all the time, and it was almost too much to bear for the Frenchman; he was convinced his colleagues thought he was stupid, and he was considering resignation. Then he observed his German colleagues for a while, and he noticed that they talked in exactly this way to each other—was everyone stupid, or is this just the way Germans talk?

In fact, how high or low context the language can also be a source of confusion and misunderstandings within cultures. As you can see from the examples above, no language gives all the information and some inside knowledge is often assumed. If we imagine the reaction of the hypothetical man from Mars, much beloved of philosophers, he would in fact understand the German's instructions best, and he might have just as much trouble with the low-context instructions for writing the report as with the high-context ones—they assume different things, but both make assumptions.

Just as cultures contain elements of both individualism and collectivism (but one tends to predominate), they also contain elements of both high-context and low-context language. Cultures vary in the specific situations in which they are prepared to accept higher- or lower-context language, as well as in the number of situations where one form or the other is appropriate. For example, giving directions in the street is a rather high-context situation in English, to the considerable frustration of tourists ('turn left where the tram depot used to be' is a favourite street direction in Brisbane). This behaviour reinforces the group membership of natives, but tends to exclude strangers. By the same token, Japanese speakers are able to 'spell things out', for example when they need to teach difficult technical material at school.

For the intercultural traveller, it is important to determine the main rules for explicitness in language that are operating in different situations, and to discover the appropriate ways—there always are appropriate ways—of obtaining more detail when this is necessary, without appearing to insult the other person or threaten the relationship. In many Western cultures, it is very appropriate to ask direct questions for more information; this can signal respect for the knowledge and expertise of the other person. In some cultures (including some groups of English speakers), however, asking questions is considered to be nosy and prying. In the case of some groups of Australian Aborigines, strangers who want information must be prepared to disclose information about themselves first; asking questions can stop the interaction altogether. With appropriate self-disclosure, the stranger will later be rewarded by getting the desired information; it just takes patience (see Eades, 1982). In fact, as in so many areas of intercultural communication, patience is crucial to dealing across high- and low-context language.

## The Functions of Language: Diglossia, Style, and Register

In Chapter 1, we pointed out that all languages have a number of forms or styles, as well as different registers for different types of situation. In addition, cultures which use more than one language (which is most of them) often use different languages for different purposes (diglossia or multiglossia; see Fishman, 1971a, 1971b). To understand the use of different languages in diglossic cultures, or the use of different styles in all cultures, we must understand the impact of the context on the speakers. As Fishman put it many years ago, to predict the type of language used, we must know who is speaking to whom, where, and when (and perhaps also why). In other words, there are social rules which govern expectations about which language or which style should or should not be used in particular situations, and by particular speakers.

The role of context is easy to see in cultures that use diglossia. For example, bilingual speakers of Spanish and Guaraní in Paraguay use Spanish in public and Guaraní at home. They use Spanish, the official language of the country, for formal situations and for dealing with official matters, but they use Guaraní for intimate conversations with friends and family members (Rubin, 1970). In other cultures, up to four or five languages can be used in this way—one for intimate conversations and at home, one for official business and school, one for church and religious matters, one for trading and business, and so forth (see Ervin-Tripp, 1971, for several interesting examples of this sort of multiglossia). In our own research, we have found evidence of subtle diglossia among bilingual Greek-Australians and Italo-Australians with respect to language (e.g., Callan & Gallois, 1982), and among a number of immigrant groups with respect to accent (e.g., Callan, Gallois & Forbes, 1983; Gallois & Callan, 1981).

In diglossic cultures, children learn both or all the languages as they become familiar with the situations in which the languages are used, and they have no more difficulty holding the languages separate than monolinguals have in holding different styles separate. This is to say they do have some problems, just as monolinguals do not always know which style to use—no language-learning task is that easy—but in general they use the different languages effectively. Their vocabulary and grammar, however, may be specific to the kinds of language they need. For example, the speakers in Paraguay we described above may not have much informal Spanish, and their formal Guaraní may also not be very good. This means that speakers from this community may have difficulties when they communicate with members of a monolingual Spanish-speaking community, where Spanish is used for everything. The same sorts of difficulties can arise, for example, when British people go to bilingual Asian communities like Singapore or Hong Kong. People in these communities are native speakers of English, but they use English for only some purposes—various Chinese languages (usually more than one) are preferred in many situations.

Whether diglossic or not, all cultures have a range of styles, which are also used in different situations and for different purposes. In some languages, like Japanese, grammar and vocabulary change across styles: Japanese speakers use different forms of words, for example, when addressing superiors and subordinates, as well as different forms for men and women. This can be very challenging for foreigners, who may have trouble coming to grips with one form of the language, let alone several. Fortunately, allowances tend to be made for non-native speakers and mistakes in the form of language are easy to explain as the mistakes of a person who is not really fluent. Indeed, Japanese people tend to believe that it is impossible for foreigners to become really fluent in their language (Hildebrandt & Giles, 1983; Ross & Shortreed, 1990), and they may automatically switch to the foreigner's language (if they are able to do so) as a consequence of these beliefs. As we will see in later chapters, this sort of belief is linked to social and cultural identity.

In fact, it is often easier to make allowances for mistakes of grammar and vocabulary than for the more subtle mistakes of style that can also occur, just because they are more obvious. Many Western languages, as we noted earlier, change styles by changing the amount of slang they include, by subtle changes in word order, by relaxing the rules of grammar in more informal situations, by changing the forms of address, and so forth. For a French speaker, it is easy to distinguish between formal language and the kind of tough but matey street language used by young people in Paris and much loved by New Wave film directors. It is not so easy, though, to put your finger on exactly *how* these styles are different—this requires a fairly sophisticated analysis, because the rules that govern such style changes exist mainly outside conscious awareness.

We will come back to style and register later, as well as discussing the differences and similarities between spoken and written languages, and how these too differ across cultures. First, however, we need to take up the other aspect of communication, which accompanies all spoken and some written language, and which can sometimes substitute for it: non-verbal communication.

## NON-VERBAL COMMUNICATION: THE MEDIUM OF FEELINGS

If language is an excellent medium for transmitting ideas, information, and beliefs, non-verbal behaviour is ideal for transmitting identity, emotions, and attitudes—who we are, how we feel, and what we think of you. While language is usually single-channel, linear in structure, and governed by strict rules of grammar and semantics, non-verbal behaviour is multichannel, non-linear, and governed by more flexible rules. In most cultures, it also has no legal force—you can be arrested and tried for saying certain things (e.g., for slander, libel, obscenity, or fraud), but, short of punching someone, you cannot usually be charged for the *way* you say it. Yet the way you say it can change the meaning of words completely. Consider the following sentence, said by a supervisor to an employee:

This report needs some more work doing on it—can you have a look at it and get back to me today?

This sentence contains a lot of information, including the description of a situation and a request/command. The meaning, in terms of the attitude of the supervisor and the nature of the request, changes greatly depending on how the sentence is said. Imagine first that the supervisor has picked up the report and is looking for help, so she gives the report to the employee for a second opinion. How would she make the request? What tone of voice, what facial expression, what sort of gestures and body movement would she be likely to use? Now imagine that the employee did the original report, and the supervisor is not pleased that it still needs work. How would her non-verbal behaviour change? Finally, imagine that the supervisor thinks the report is great, and with a little more work will be exactly what the department needs. How will she get this across, using the sentence above?

It would be easy to convey any of these complex messages, and indeed a number of other ones, using the words above.

We do this kind of thing constantly, although we may not always be aware of it. In fact, non-verbal behaviour is produced even more automatically than words (Argyle, 1988), and the cultural and social rules that determine much of it may be difficult to verbalise. In many contexts, however, it is non-verbal behaviour that determines the meaning. For example, Noller (1984) found that in conversations between spouses, only about 30 per cent of the language could be coded as emotionally positive or negative, but when non-verbal behaviour was included, more than 70 per cent of the communication had a positive or negative tone. Thus, it is important for intercultural travellers to look at the way non-verbal communication is structured, and how it differs across cultures.

## Channels of Communication

One of the most interesting features of non-verbal communication is that it is multichannel: the message is conveyed using the voice, face, and body, and often all three are conveying more-or-less the same emotion or attitude. This is fortunate, as people in conversation often attend mainly to the words, and do not pay much attention to the non-verbal behaviour—especially if they are American or Western European. People studying non-verbal communication describe anywhere from five to 25 channels, depending on their perspective; in the next paragraphs, we discuss six channels, which we believe capture the main channels of communication, especially those that differ across cultures.

As we describe the channels of communication, we will emphasise three dimensions which have been found by many researchers to be universal across cultures; one or more of them applies to virtually every communication situation (see Argyle, 1988; Osgood, May & Miron, 1975; Russell, 1991; Scherer, 1988). The first of these is positive–negative (sometimes called *evaluation, affiliation,* or *solidarity*), which indicates how much we like something (or don't like it) and how friendly or unfriendly we feel towards another person or group. The second dimension is dominant–submissive (usually called *power*), and indicates how much we feel in control of a situation or another person, or how much we feel controlled by the other; this dimension is especially important when we communicate in organisational settings. The third dimension is active–passive (often called *arousal*, *activity*, or *involvement*), and indicates how interested or excited (or, alternatively, how bored) we are by a situation or person.

### *Voice*

The voice is frequently forgotten when non-verbal behaviour is considered, as the voice is the main medium for transmitting verbal behaviour (language), at least in conversation. Along with the words we speak, however, comes another part of the voice which communicates feelings, attitudes, and identity (see Pittam, 1994). This non-verbal behaviour is sometimes referred to as *tone of voice*, and includes the pitch (high to low) at which we speak, volume (soft to loud), speed (fast to slow), tension (relaxed to tense), variation (monotonous to variable), enunciation (slurred to precise), and a number of voice qualities (e.g., breathiness, whisper, creakiness) that modify the meaning of words. In addition, the voice contains some features of language, including accent, which are important in signalling cultural identity, and about which we will have more to say in a later chapter. In fact, it is no exaggeration to say that the words and the voice together contain all the essential verbal and non-verbal information we need to communicate. This feature of the voice is demonstrated very well in telephone conversations.

All cultures have stereotypes about what particular vocal features and qualities mean. In American English, for example, loud, low-pitched, and fast speech is interpreted as dominant behaviour. In German, on the other hand, dominance is signalled by low pitch, soft volume, and breathiness, at least when the speaker is male (Scherer,1979). Other cultures have still different stereotypes of dominance in the voice. The same thing applies to positivity (signalled in European American English by soft volume and breathiness) and arousal (signalled by loud volume, relatively high pitch, high speed, and vocal tension). Given these American stereotypes, it is not surprising that British speakers of English often believe Americans are highly extroverted and excitable; their own stereotypes for dominance and involvement involve slower speech and in particular softer volume. Once again, each culture has its own vocal stereotypes, although all of them can be well-described using the dimensions of positivity, dominance, and arousal. Members of each culture tend to interpret others as if they were following the rules for vocal communication of the home culture.

### Gaze

If the voice and the words carry all the information we need to understand another speaker, the words and the body (or non-vocal behaviour) also carry everything we need, a feature of communication that was exploited in the past by the directors of silent films. One of the most important channels of non-vocal behaviour is gaze or eye contact. This channel is unique in that, by looking at another person, we simultaneously send the other person information about how we feel and put ourselves in a position to take in information about the other person. On the other hand, real eye contact (looking directly into another person's eyes) is quite physiologically arousing, and many speakers avoid doing this for more than a few seconds at a time, except in very intimate relationships (see Argyle, 1988).

For English speakers, gaze tends to occur more while the person is listening than while the person is speaking; speakers often look away while constructing their speech. Stereotypes about gaze among Anglo-Celtic people associate a lot of gaze with liking for the other person, respect for the other person, and high involvement in the interaction—looking away most of the time means boredom, disrespect, or dislike (an exception to this is the stare of people competing for dominance). In a large number of other cultures and sub-cultures (including African Americans), however, the stereotypes about gaze are almost opposite to this—in particular, respect is signalled by looking down. As you can see, the same channel is conveying the same message, but in a different way.

### Facial expression

When we are in conversation, we tend to pay more attention to the face, which is where speech comes from and where the eyes are, than to the rest of the body. As a result, we tend to be more accurate in making judgements about emotion and deception based on facial expression than based on body movement (see Ekman, 1982; Rosenthal, 1979). One extremely important aspect of facial expression that appears to be universal across cultures is the expression of strong, basic emotions—in particular happiness, surprise, contempt, disgust, fear, anger, and sadness. Scherer and his colleagues have found evidence that this may also be true for the voice (see Scherer, 1988). Ekman and his colleagues have described these expressions in a large number of cultures, and have shown that people are very accurate at guessing which emotion is being expressed, even when the person expressing the emotion is from a very distant culture. Three main parts of the face—the forehead and eyebrows, the eyes, and the mouth— are involved, and the basic emotions are expressed roughly in the following ways:

*Happiness:* smiling mouth, puffed lower eyelids, smooth brow and forehead.
*Surprise:* raised eyebrows, wide-open eyes, open mouth.
*Contempt:* lowered brow, narrowed eyes, closed mouth.
*Disgust:* brow lowered and drawn inwards, upper lip raised, which sometimes causes the nose to wrinkle.
*Fear:* brow raised, furrowed, and drawn inwards, wide-open eyes, mouth open with lips drawn back.

*Anger:* lowered brow, staring (sometimes narrowed) eyes, jaw clenched, mouth either closed or open with teeth bared.

*Sadness:* brow lowered (sometimes drawn inward), inside corners of lower eyelid raised, corners of the mouth pulled down.

Ekman and Friesen (1975) demonstrate that these expressions can become more or less intense with more or less intense emotions, but the basic expression remains the same. In addition, some recent research suggests that putting our faces in the positions that express these emotions (particularly happiness) can actually change our mood (Cappella, 1993; Zajonc, Murphy & Inglehart, 1989). It is some comfort also to know that these basic emotions are very easy to pick in other people from our own and different cultures. Indeed, even tiny babies have all these expressions in their repertoire of non-verbal communication.

The problem comes when we realise that we do not in fact express strong, basic emotions very often, with the possible exception of happiness. Ask yourself, for example, how many times in the past you have used the basic expression for fear (we hope not at all)—for anger—for disgust. How many times have you seen other people use them? Most of the time, the emotions people express are not very intense, and in addition are mixtures of two or more of these basic emotions: apprehension, for example, is a blend of surprise and mild fear; annoyance is a complex blend of anger, contempt, and sometimes sadness (see Ekman & Friesen, 1975). On top of this, we may try to disguise the way we are feeling by neutralising our facial expression (using a 'poker face'), or by covering the emotion we feel with another emotion—looking happy, for example, even when we are angry with another person. In this case, the real emotion may leak through in our face or in some other non-verbal channel (for example, the voice or the way we move our bodies). In fact, guessing how another person feels when the emotion is complex is a subtle social skill (see Argyle, 1988, and Gallois, 1993, for more detailed discussions of these issues, including differences across cultures).

All cultures have rules about when, where, how, and how much different emotions can be expressed (Argyle, 1988; Scherer, 1988). As we noted in Chapter 1, these rules are related to the value of individualism–collectivism (see Markus & Kitayama, 1991). Individualist cultures, where people tend to have more independent self-concepts, also encourage the expression of most emotions in public. Of course, there are differences in individualist cultures about how much different emotions can be expressed, depending upon the sex of the speaker—women are expected to be more expressive (see Hall, 1979; Lutz, 1990)—the status of the person, and the situation. Nevertheless, in collectivist cultures, where people tend to have more interdependent self-concepts, the expression of strong emotions in public, especially negative emotions, is often suppressed in the interests of harmony (Ekman, 1972). This means, for example, it is harder to guess the way a Japanese person feels from facial expression than a British or Italian person—even when the person doing the guessing is also Japanese (Argyle, Shimoda & Ricci-Bitti, 1978). One important reason that Japanese and Chinese people appear 'inscrutable' to Western Europeans comes from the rules in these cultures prohibiting the expression of emotions in public.

### *Gestures*

We move our hands and feet almost constantly when we speak, as a way of emphasising, illustrating, and embellishing the words we say, as well as to express nervousness, excitement, anxiety, and other emotions (see Ekman & Friesen, 1969, for a detailed discussion of the use of gestures). Some hand gestures, called *emblems*, are used as substitutes for words (we discussed emblems in Chapter 1); these gestures really should be considered as part of language. As we noted earlier, the same gestures can mean different things even in closely related cultures, just as the same sounds can mean different things. In addition, some cultures have taboos on gestures that do not exist in other cultures. For example, in many cultures it is insulting to point with the index finger at another person, while in other cultures this is perfectly acceptable behaviour. Fortunately, it is relatively easy to learn the rules about emblems in a new culture, because they are quite explicit. The best rule for intercultural travellers is this: *say it with words rather than gestures until you know the rules. and say it carefully.* You can learn which emblems are acceptable by watching what other people do and do not do.

Those gestures which are genuine non-verbal behaviour—the ones which accompany words but which convey how we feel or what our attitude is—are harder to explain and understand, even in our home culture. For one thing, there are large individual differences in the amount people gesture, and sex, age, family background, and personality traits like extroversion all influence this behaviour (see Buck, 1988; Lanzetta, Cartwright-Smith & Kleck, 1976; Tannen, 1986). There are also large cultural differences. One of the earliest researchers in non-verbal communication (Efron, 1941) looked at gestures among Anglo-Americans, Jews from Eastern Europe, and Italians in New York City. Efron found that Italians tended to gesture using the whole arm from the shoulder down, Jews gestured using the lower half of the arm only, and Anglo-Americans used mainly the hand and wrist. People from all three cultural groups who were born in the USA, however, came closer to following the rules for Anglo-Americans. Thus, it appeared that members of immigrant groups assimilated with their gestures as well as in other ways. More recently, we found few differences in the gestural patterns of Italian immigrants in Australia and native speakers, in spite of stereotypes about their greater level of gesturing (Gallois & Callan, 1986, 1988), probably because these people had lived in Australia for years and had accommodated to the behaviour of native speakers, much as had the second-generation people in Efron's work.

Stereotypes about gestures, like stereotypes about the voice and other kinds of non-verbal behaviour, also vary across cultures. In Britain, for example, large gestures are interpreted as highly aroused and dominant—excited, perhaps even angry. Thus, it is not hard to understand the impression of many British people that Italians are in a constant state of high excitement—and the converse impression on the part of Italians that Britishers are very reserved, 'cold fish'. The same emotions and attitudes are conveyed by gestures of different sizes, so that, for a British speaker, a little bit of gesture goes a long way, while, for an Italian, small gestures may hardly be noticed at all.

### Touch

The world seems to be divided into cultures that touch and cultures that do not touch (Hall, 1959). It goes without saying that people in every culture touch some people (lovers, family members) in some situations, especially in private; in fact, humans as a species have a basic need for this kind of physical contact. Nevertheless, there are strong taboos in many cultures about touching at all, particularly in public. For example, many years ago Jourard (1966) observed young couples sitting and talking in cafes in London, Gainesville, Florida, Paris, and San Juan, Puerto Rico. In San Juan, the couples touched on average 180 times in an hour, and in Paris, they touched almost as often. In Gainesville, however, he observed an average of two touches in an hour, and in London, none at all. While we would probably find smaller differences today, this is the kind of strong difference that exists between touch and non-touch cultures.

Because of the rules they have about touch, people in different cultures also give different meanings to touch. For a Britisher or European American, for example, a light touch with the hand on another person's arm or back carries great impact, especially if the people are not the same sex. In the USA, Henley (1977) noted that these kinds of touches are usually initiated by more powerful people, and she interpreted them as signals of dominance and power. In cultures where touch is common (e.g., Latin American, southern European, and Arab cultures), however, such touches may hardly be noticed—you have to hug the other person to show affection, for example. On the other hand, people in these cultures notice the absence of touch, and interpret it as coldness or hostility.

### *Distance and orientation*

In Chapter 2, we gave some examples of cultural differences in the distances people stand from each other and the way they orient their bodies to each other. Most of us do not think of distance and orientation as very important as a communication channel, yet E.T. Hall (1966) showed that cultures have very strict rules about the appropriate distance and orientation to take, and that these rules are associated with important cultural values about respect, dominance, and intimacy (see also Hayduk, 1978, 1983).

In the USA, in most of Western Europe and in Australia, informal conversations take place with a speaker-to-speaker orientation of approximately 45 degrees and at a distance of 0.5 to 1 metre; closer distances are for intimate conversations, while more formal conversations can involve distances up to 3 metres. In the Arab world and in Latin America, the rules are similar, but the distances are much shorter, while body orientation is more face-to-face. In Chinese culture, the distances tend to be greater and the orientation more side-by-side. Interestingly enough, however, Chinese people do not have a problem with tolerating very small distances in non-conversational settings like queues and crowded rooms. British visitors are often very surprised that the Chinese person who backs away from them in conversation walks so close to them in a restaurant that their bodies nearly touch at many points. As is so often the case for nonverbal behaviour, the rules are different from one situation to another, and the same behaviour carries a different meaning.

## Many Channels, One Communication Package

The last few pages may have left your head spinning, as they are a long catalogue of behaviours for you to consider. There are different meanings in different situations, for different people, and in different cultures. In fact, the catalogue could have been much longer; we have only touched the surface of what is known about non-verbal behaviour (see Argyle, 1988; Burgoon, Buller & Woodall, 1995; Feldman, 1992, for more comprehensive reviews). As you can see from the research we describe, this area has a long history, and the findings about cultural differences are in many cases very well established.

What does not come through clearly when one channel of communication at a time is described is that all the channels combine to produce a complex communicative message. Even though, in general, words are used to convey information, whereas the non-verbal channels are used to convey identity, attitudes, and feelings, words can be used to convey these things too. When they are, the feeling or attitude comes across as very definite or strong, and we must be prepared to own it. That is why many people prefer to express emotions and attitudes—particularly anger, fear, or refusal—as non-verbally as they can. Once again, this is especially true in collectivist cultures, where a subtle hint of anger or displeasure can get the message across without threatening the relationship, but a more direct verbal or even non-verbal statement could be risky.

Sometimes the words, the voice, the eyes, the face, and the body are all giving essentially the same message; imagine the lover who says 'I love you' on all channels at once, or the supervisor who does the same thing with 'You're fired!'. In many cases, however, different messages are sent on different channels, to produce a more complex, subtle, or ambiguous package. Think of sarcasm (for example, saying 'He's just wonderful!' with a contemptuous facial expression and a nasal, monotonous tone of voice), teasing (saying 'You're in *big* trouble!' with a smile and a pat on the back) as clearcut cases where contradictory messages are deliberately sent to produce a complex message. At other times, attitudes or emotions leak through in spite of our attempts to control them, and the message becomes ambiguous as a result. Imagine, for example, the teacher who says to a student, 'That's good work!', with a positive tone of voice but a worried facial expression. Does the student believe the positive voice or the negative face? (Probably the latter, as a large number of studies have shown; see, e.g., Bugental, 1993.)

Sending and receiving messages on the non-verbal channels is therefore a subtle social skill that is learned within a culture over many years—usually without being explicitly taught— and some people learn these skills better than others (see Riggio, 1986; Rosenthal et al., 1978). In addition, people in the same culture misunderstand each other very frequently as a result of misinterpretations of non-verbal behaviour (see Tannen, 1986, 1990). Many authors, starting with E.T. Hall, have advised making the non-verbal behaviour verbal or using words instead of gestures as a way of repairing these misunderstandings. By bringing attitudes and emotions to the surface in communication terms, and by taking responsibility for them, it can be easier to acknowledge and correct mistakes. In addition, verbalising our attitudes and emotions slows down the communication process, making it easier not to jump to conclusions about what another person means before we have considered all the alternative possibilities.

## CONCLUSIONS AND STRATEGIES

So what is a well-intentioned traveller to do when faced with communicating across cultures, or indeed across sub-cultures within a single culture? For one thing, there is not much point in trying to learn all the differences in language and non-verbal communication that exist across the cultural groups, as this will take more years than most of us can afford. Instead, the same kinds of strategies that we presented in the first two chapters can also be put to use here, as they have specific applications for dealing with cultural differences in language and non-verbal behaviour. Here is a set of guidelines for you to think about:

1. Keep an open mind—people may not mean the same thing you mean by particular words or non-verbal behaviour. Never, never, NEVER assume you know what other people mean, or that they must know what you mean.
2. Remember that, even though strong, basic emotions are expressed in the same way everywhere, most of the time people are expressing weak, complex emotions, and there are many differences across cultures.
3. Watch what other people do—if they are treating everyone the same way as they are treating you, this probably means that you are observing a general rule in this culture.
4. Remember that all cultures have ways of expressing positivity, dominance, and arousal—they just don't all do it in the same way. Watch friends and enemies, superiors and subordinates, and bored and interested people to find out how they do it.
5. Be prepared to explain what you say and do in more detail than would be necessary in your own culture. Others may not know your culture's rules, and they may make surprising assumptions about your behaviour.
6. Be ready to ask if you don't understand why someone did something in a certain way, or said something in a certain way. Find out the appropriate ways of asking first; however—once again—it pays to observe.
7. Be patient and expect to make mistakes. There are very few mistakes which cannot be repaired.

This last point brings us to the subject of politeness, face-saving, and communication repair. The next chapter takes up these issues in more detail, especially in public situations like work and dealing with clients and customers. Remember that, in our home cultures, working life is a nearly-constant process of communication repair by one person or another. When the normal difficulties of communication are overlaid with differences in cultural rules, misunderstandings are not likely to diminish, so it is important not to get too upset when they occur. This can be difficult, as we noted earlier, because intercultural travel is stressful in itself, and misunderstandings are especially likely to be upsetting. Thus, it is worth becoming very familiar with misunderstandings in your own group and in your own home culture, so that the intercultural ones do not come as so much of a surprise.

# 4

# CULTURE, SELF-EXPRESSION, AND MAINTAINING RELATIONSHIPS

In this chapter, we will explore in more detail the consequences of social rules. We will concentrate on social and work situations that tend to cause discomfort, tension, or difficulty, and that are often problematic for professionals in dealing with colleagues, clients, or customers from other cultures. Given the functions of social rules (cf. Argyle, Furnham & Graham, 1981):

— to express oneself and defend one's own beliefs
— to avoid conflict
— to maintain relationships

it is not surprising that difficult situations occur. We need to be aware of how to repair misunderstandings, to preserve the self-respect of others (as well as one's own self-respect) after a mistake, and to manage conflict. Each of these situations is governed especially strongly by social rules, and rule violations in such situations can have very serious consequences. In the first section, we take up the issue of being polite.

## SOCIAL RULES ABOUT POLITENESS

One of the social rules that is found to be universal across situations and common across many cultures is 'behave politely' (Argyle, Furnham & Graham, 1981; Argyle et al., 1986). What counts as polite, however, may not be the same in all cultures or in all situations. For example, it is perfectly polite (i.e., not rule-violating) in many cultures to treat a close friend or family member with great familiarity. In some cultures, this same familiarity (use of first name or a nickname, use of slang, use of touch) can extend to close friends at work and to students at university or in adult education programmes. In other cultures, however, such people expect to be treated more formally. Even closely related cultures differ in these politeness rules. For example, Britons tend to treat people more formally in work situations than do Americans or Australians, and French people tend to be more formal than Belgians or Franco-Canadians. In each culture, though, it is clear to people when rules about politeness are being broken.

## Forms of Address

Politeness rules influence every aspect of communication, starting with the appropriate way to address others. Ervin-Tripp (1971) catalogued the rules for address current in the USA during the 1960s. For example, she noted that there are certain situations, such as courtrooms, doctors' offices, and the like, where the appropriate form of address may be a title only ('Your Honour', 'Doctor', etc.), and no first or family name is used. Such situations occur in most cultures, but they are relatively uncommon and tend to be fairly formal.

A major rule for forms of address in the USA, Ervin-Tripp (1971) noted, is age: Americans address younger people (i.e., people 15 years or more younger than they are themselves) by their first name ('Sally'), but usually receive title plus last name back ('Mr Smith'). This same rule is often applied at work where power is unequal. For example, American teachers are usually called by title plus last name by their students (in other cultures, this form may be title only: 'Miss' or 'Sir' in the UK and Australia), but they call their students by their first name (or last name only in some British schools). In all these situations, the more powerful (or older) person has the right to give permission for the other person to use first name only. This permission may be given explicitly. For example, a university professor may tell his class, 'Call me Roger'; otherwise, they may address him as 'Professor Brown'. Permission may also be given implicitly; for example, the more powerful person may introduce herself as 'Marie Davis' after being introduced by someone else as 'Dr Davis'.

The expression of an unequal distribution of power can go beyond the name used to address another person. In a classic case, Brown and Gilman (1960) studied the use of the pronoun 'you' in many European cultures. This pronoun in most languages has a formal form ('vous' in French, 'Sie' in German, 'usted' in Spanish), and a familiar form ('tu', 'du', and 'tu' in these three languages); this was also the case in English in the past ('you' and 'thou'). They found that the non-reciprocal use of 'you' commonly signalled a difference in power; the formal form was used in the upward direction, and the familiar form was used for downward communication. In recent times, this usage has decreased in most European languages. These days, the formal form of 'you' tends to be used to signal a formal relationship (for example, doctor–patient, lawyer–client, or work colleagues), while the familiar form signals more intimate relationships (family members or close friends).

It goes almost without saying that rules like these cause some confusion about what to call people. For example, a university student may be visiting a counsellor for help with study skills. The counsellor, who is only a little older than the student, calls her 'Susanne' from the first meeting. What does the student call the counsellor? 'Ms Green' may seem too formal, given the similarity in age, but 'Janet' may be too familiar, given the counsellor's role. If Janet Green does not give any indication of what she wants to be called, the student is likely not to use any name at all. In fact, it is not unusual for people in these sorts of role relationships to go on for months without calling one another by any name, which can make situations such as telephone calls and public meetings rather awkward, to say the least.

Add to this ambiguity the differences between cultures in forms of address, and the confusion is multiplied. Cultures that are higher in power distance are more likely to use, and to continue using for a longer period of time, the kind of non-reciprocal forms of address noted above for students and teachers. Cultures that avoid uncertainty may retain formal forms of address for a long time. For example, it is not uncommon for work colleagues in France to address each other as 'M. Dupont' and 'Mme Clément', and to call each other 'vous', for 20 or 30 years. Note, though, that this is not the case for all speakers of French. In Belgium, such colleagues are more likely to address each other by first name and to call each other 'tu'. In addition, the rules about forms of address are stricter in some cultures than in others. Americans, for example, are relatively relaxed about mistakes in this area, but people in some cultures find it very offensive to be called by the 'wrong' name.

What, then, is the intercultural traveller to do, when the rules change between cultures and when there is so much ambiguity in any case? Once again, our strategy is the same as in other contexts:

1. Watch what others do, and try to imitate them.
2. Wait for a signal from the other person—with any luck, that person will tell you what he or she wants to be called.
3. In general, use the form of 'you' (in languages where there is a choice) that the other person uses with you.
4. If all else fails, use the 'no-name' strategy, but try to resolve the situation as soon as you can—this is a temporary solution at best.

Remember that forms of address are a signal of the type of relationship you have with the other person. There is more involved here than just a name. The name you use carries a strong message about the power between you and that other person, as well as the friendship and solidarity you have for him or her.

## Polite Style and Register

Like forms of address, the formality of the style, including both language and non-verbal behaviour, and the register used signal a great deal about the situation and the relationship between people, and the rules for style and register are often very important. If, when you go to the garage to get your car repaired, your language is too formal or you use your professional register (complete with technical terms), you may be seen as patronising or 'too posh' by the mechanics. In Australia, this can translate into lack of service or worse. On the other hand, the mechanics may be quite ready to use their own technical register, leading their customers to feel confused and frustrated; patients often complain of this same kind of behaviour from their doctors. We all have a range of styles and registers, at least in our native language, but we may not be comfortable using many of them.

Many languages, as we noted in Chapter 3, mark style and register very clearly. For example, Japanese uses different language forms for addressing people of higher and lower status, and for men and women. The advantage of this strict marking is that once the styles and registers are learned, there is little ambiguity about how to speak in these different relationships. In Western languages (English in particular), register and especially style change according to more implicit social rules, which are often only partly in the conscious awareness of speakers. Nevertheless, gross violations of these rules can lead to misunderstanding and sometimes hostility or dislike, even if the person who makes the mistake comes from another culture. For example, an American businessman may pat a new customer on the back as a signal of friendliness, and although this gesture may be taken as far too informal by people from many other cultures, it may nevertheless be appreciated in high-touch cultures in Latin America or the Middle East if the customer is also a man.

Rules about polite and appropriate style and register are subtle. They vary according to the group membership and the relationship between people. A number of researchers (e.g., Horvath, 1985; Trudgill, 1986) have found, for example, that women tend to use more formal style (including more of the high language forms, standard grammar, and prestige pronunciations) than men do, and men may believe that they must speak more formally (for example, using less slang and making sure they pronounce words 'correctly' (e.g., 'going', not 'goin' '). Unfortunately, in many work settings professional women feel strongly that they should not be talked to differently from men, and they may even go out of their way to use informal language, slang, and even four-letter words. This clash of rules and stereotypes can lead men (and women as well) to believe that they can't win. If they are too formal, they are criticised; and if they are too informal, the other person is insulted.

There is some truth to this belief. Like forms of address, style and register are important signals of the context and the relationship. When people disagree about the appropriate style or register to use, their behaviour may be masking a disagreement about division of power in the relationship or about how friendly they really are (cf. Gumperz, 1982; Henley & Kramarae, 1991). Sometimes, however, one person has made a genuine mistake, and it is important to keep this possibility in mind, particularly when people from different cultures are talking. It is important not to jump to conclusions when another person uses a style or register that seems inappropriate. One plausible explanation is that the other person thinks the style is appropriate, and another is that the person knows only that style; that is, the person is not familiar enough with the rules of the language and culture to switch styles easily. Similarly, if your behaviour produces an unexpected reaction in a person from another culture, you should keep an open mind to the possibility that you have violated one of that culture's important rules. You can defuse the situation by asking if you have done something wrong—this gives other people an easy way to tell you why they are uncomfortable or upset. If this happens, you can then explain why you did what you did, and apologise for upsetting the other person.

## Face and Politeness

Rules about politeness are especially important when there has been miscommunication, or when someone has made an error of judgement about communication. For example, imagine the following scene: You are a doctor treating a patient for the first time. You take a history, examine the patient, note a small health problem, and begin to discuss the treatment and management of this problem. Suddenly, out of nowhere, the patient asks you a very personal question, in a way that indicates to you that she is very distressed. How do you feel? What do you do? How do you handle this situation with the least possible damage to yourself and to the patient?

This scene illustrates a threat to your self-respect, self-esteem, or privacy. Brown and Levinson (1978, 1987), in their work on politeness, have referred to this kind of thing as a threat to *negative face*, or a person's desire (right) not to be imposed upon. They contrast negative face to *positive face*, or a person's desire to be well regarded and seen in a positive light. These authors argue that in public life (including life at work) we are strongly motivated to maintain both our positive and negative face, and as a result we cooperate with others in maintaining their face too. Thus, in the scene above, if you (as the doctor) respond too harshly, you may make the patient look stupid or feel ashamed, and thus threaten her positive face, which may violate social rules about politeness. Very often, indeed, threats to the negative face of one person are associated with potential threats to the positive face of another.

How do you handle such a threat, a potential invasion of your privacy? You have, of course, a number of options, as Brown and Levinson (1987) discuss. First, you can respond directly and without frills, along the lines of 'I don't intend to answer such a personal question; you shouldn't have asked it!' This *bald on-record* response protects your negative face (i.e., reduces the threat to your privacy), but it also threatens the patient's positive face by criticising her behaviour. Alternatively, you can go *off-record*, by giving an evasive answer to the question, which may satisfy her. In this way, you save her face, but you may not succeed in reducing the threat to your own. Finally, you may adopt one of several *politeness* strategies. You could refuse to answer, but add some flattering statement to protect her positive face ('you are such an intelligent person, you will understand'). Alternatively, you could use answer in a way that would address the patient's negative face (such as, 'I can understand why you ask, but I can't answer that question')—or you could do both. You may also be able to use non-verbal behaviour (smiling, looking directly at the patient, leaning forward—all signals of friendliness and interest) to soften the refusal and enhance the politeness strategy you use (see Burgoon, Stern & Dillman, 1995). In general, the more you use politeness, particularly the sort of politeness that addresses the face threat to the other person, the more you will minimise the negative consequences for the relationship.

Which of these strategies—ranging from the least polite, bald on-record comment, through the politeness strategies to off-record comments (which may not get the message across at all)—should you choose in this situation? That will depend on a number of factors, including the type of relationship you have with the other person who, in this case, is a new patient. Rakos (1991) argues that the closer and longer the relationship, the more we are obligated not to offend the other person or not to threaten the other person's face. A second consideration, however, is the potential length of the relationship. In this case, the patient could potentially become a regular. Thirdly, it is important to consider the threat to your own face, and the importance you attach to it. The more you are concerned about the invasion of privacy, the more you need to get across a clear message about it. The doctor in this example, in fact, could choose any of the strategies. Bald on-record comment would almost certainly stop the questioning. This response reflects the social power that doctors have in interviews with patients, and thus might not put the patient off too much. On the other hand, comment accompanied by positive or negative politeness is likely to be effective also, and not to be so threatening to the patient. The important thing to remember is that there is a choice, and you should make it in full consideration of the possible consequences.

Let us continue this example for a little longer. Imagine that the new patient who asked the very personal question comes from another culture. What difference is this likely to make in terms of how you (as the doctor) feel about the personal question, and what difference is your response likely to make to her? By now, you should have a fairly strong intuition about the answers to these questions. One major difference is that, because this is an intercultural encounter, it is more likely that the doctor and the patient will have different ideas, and different rules, about what is and is not appropriate in their interview. The patient may believe, for instance, that personal questions to the doctor are within the range of appropriate options for her. She is likely to think this if her culture constructs doctor–patient relationships more as family relationships than does your culture. It is also possible that you, given your own rules for the way questions in medical interviews should be asked, may think the question is more personal than she intended it to be. Thus, you and the patient may well have different ideas about how impolite her behaviour is (if it is impolite at all).

In addition, you and the patient are very likely to have different rules about what counts as positive and negative politeness. Remember the example in Chapter 1, where Paul (the Dutch colleague) believed that direct expression of criticism was perfectly appropriate, whereas Jane (the Australian colleague) felt it should be hedged in polite qualifications. This was, in fact, a disagreement about what constitutes a threat to face (Jane thought it was, Paul didn't), and what sorts of polite words would reduce the threat. For Jane, the polite words were essential, while, for Paul, they took the criticism off-record and he didn't hear it at all. So the patient may not interpret your polite response in the way it was intended either, because her rules are different.

Politeness and face, like so much of communication, are closely tied to cultural values. For high power-distance cultures, more politeness is necessary when the other person is higher in status or power than when the other is lower power; in low power–distance cultures, the rules about politeness tend to be more reciprocal. Sometimes, the rules are even stricter for higher-power people than for lower-power ones. For example, in Australia, Bryan and Gallois (1992) found that the rules for supervisors about giving feedback and asking for extra help were stricter and involved more indirect talk than they did for subordinates—a clear example of *noblesse oblige* in this individualist and low power-distance culture. In addition, collectivist cultures may have politeness rules that are more attuned to maintaining group harmony and less attuned to maintaining the face, especially the negative face, of individual people. Thus, Matsumoto (1994) concludes that negative politeness does not have currency in the Japanese context. Overall, if you can learn these rules, you will have learned a great deal of helpful information about the culture; this also applies to making explicit the rules about face and politeness in your own culture.

## Assertive Communication: Self-defence and Respect for Others

At first glance, assertive communication may not seem to be connected to face maintenance and politeness, but in fact the rules governing them have much in common, and the kinds of cross-cultural and sub-cultural differences that arise with other forms of polite communication also appear for assertiveness. In the early days of the assertiveness training movement, assertiveness was defined as a form of emotional expressiveness, the direct communication of feelings and desires (see Wolpe, 1958). Strange as it may seem, given today's sex-role stereotypes, women were thought in the 1940s to have special difficulties in expressing their emotions directly. The prevalence of this belief about women in the West tells us something about the role of cultural stereotypes in every kind of communication. Because of it, there was an early and continuing emphasis on assertion training for women.

In the 1970s, the concept of assertiveness and the assertion training movement, particularly in the USA, were strongly influenced by the attitudes of the times: pragmatism; strong individualism with the consequent belief that people should own their own desires, beliefs, and feelings; cultural relativism (in this case, the view that I have as much right to my beliefs as you do to yours, and vice versa), and an assumption that all people are equal, or at least can treat each other as if they were (Rakos, 1991). The definition of assertive communication was expanded to something like this (adapted from Lange & Jakubowksi, 1976): *direct expression of thoughts, desires, and feelings, without violating the rights of others.* As before, there was a strong emphasis on women's difficulties in asserting their desires, so much so that some people began to complain that the very concept of assertion was gender-bound, stressing male values in the Western context (Crawford, 1988). In addition, assertion was thought by many laypeople to be 'polite aggression'; some people, indeed, have difficulty in telling assertion and aggression apart.

In the past decade, it has become clear that assertive communication is not something you can turn on and off at need,
like a water tap. In fact, people trained in assertive communication have increasingly reported unexpected negative consequences of their behaviour—sudden hostility from close
friends and family, being sacked from their jobs by
employers—which has led many to abandon this behaviour
as too dangerous. Problems like these led Furnham (1983) to
describe the transfer of new communication skills like assertiveness out of the training environment and into real life as
the 'Achilles' heel' of the whole social skills training movement. As we have learned more about assertiveness, it has
become increasingly obvious that this type of communication
is governed by strongly held social rules, including rules
about politeness (see Rakos, 1991; Wilson & Gallois, 1993).

If you think about it, standard assertive communication sounds
very similar to bald on-record comment (Brown & Levinson,
1987). For instance, a recommended response to a salesman who
is trying to persuade or pressure you to buy something you
don't want is, 'I understand, but I'm not interested'. There is not
much here to help maintain the positive or negative face of the
other person. This response may be effective enough in a short-
term relationship with no future, such as a customer in a shop.
Most people, however, are more interested in communicating
effectively in their work and personal relationships, which are
ongoing and involve an exchange of benefits and obligations. In
such a case, it may be more important to maintain the relationship and avoid conflict (two important functions of social rules)
than to express what you really feel or think.

On the other hand, you may want to express yourself *and also*
avoid threats to the relationship. In this case, you need to be
aware of the social rules that govern assertive communication.
These rules, as it turns out, are very similar to the rules about
face and politeness described in the previous section. On-record
assertive comments accompanied by friendly non-verbal behaviour and statements of understanding (sometimes called

assertion with empathy) are often very effective in getting what you want, but less threatening to the other person, than straight assertive statements (St Lawrence et al., 1985). In addition, Wilson and Gallois (1993) found that men and women knew the social rules surrounding assertive communication and believed that it was important to use them, as a way of showing respect and consideration for the other person. For example, they found that when you refuse a request, it is important to give a reason. Standard assertion training says you are under no obligation to do this, but in many cultures there are strongly held social rules that say you should. Following the rules is seen as the most effective strategy of all (Wilson, Whicker & Price, 1994).

Rules about assertion are tied to rules about politeness and to cultural values. For example, Chinese managers in Hong Kong appear to advocate aggressive behaviour, especially by the more powerful people in the group, rather than assertive behaviour, to resolve serious conflicts (Bond & Forgas, 1984). European and African Americans have different rules about assertive behaviour, and they are also more likely to interpret such behaviour as aggressive if it comes from a person of the other race (Hrop & Rakos, 1985). In general, in intercultural encounters it is especially important to be aware that the kinds of contexts where we feel a need to be assertive—negotiations, conflicts, giving feedback to others about their behaviour— tend to be stressful and ambiguous, and thus to be governed by important rules about appropriate behaviour and politeness. These are just the kinds of contexts where intercultural misunderstandings are the most likely, so they are the contexts where it is most important to slow down and think about the communication process as well as the desired outcomes.

## CONVERSATIONS AND OTHER WAYS OF USING LANGUAGE

When we think of language, the first thing that comes to mind is usually speech in face-to-face conversations. For most of us, face-to-face conversation is *real* communication; other forms seem somehow inferior. In the previous chapter, our discussion of non-verbal communication implicitly assumed that the communication was face-to-face, and the discussion of face and politeness in this chapter has assumed the same thing. At present, of course, we rely increasingly on other forms of communication, including telephone and teleconference, letters, memos, faxes, and e-mail—in the future, many of us will add videoconferencing, electronic bulletin boards, and the World Wide Web to our repertoire, if we don't already use them. These other forms of communication are especially likely to occur in intercultural encounters. If the business has an office in Hong Kong, we may only rarely see our colleagues there, when we or they make a visit. At all other times we must rely on written or telephone communication. This means that for many people, particularly in multinational companies, face-to-face conversation is no longer the main way communication at work takes place.

In the modern workplace, we need to think about the rules for mediated communication as well as face-to-face interactions. Are these rules the same, or are there differences we need to understand? How are cultural values reflected in written language, and in communication using new technologies? What additional problems or possibilities for misunderstanding does mediated communication bring, and how can these challenges be addressed? We will spend the remainder of this chapter dealing with these issues.

## Spoken and Written Language

What difference does it make whether we speak to a colleague or a customer face-to-face, or whether we communicate in another medium? One obvious difference is in the possibilities for non-verbal communication. Another difference, however, is in the impact of spoken as compared to written language. In the past, people in most literate cultures have used writing for their most formal and committed communication. Writing is especially formal in those cultures which do not employ alphabetic writing (for example, languages whose written form uses Chinese ideographs, like the Chinese languages, Japanese, and Korean). Contracts, laws, official documents of other kinds are all written down and signed to show that they have been agreed. Many of these documents have the force of law, which means that negotiators and others are often reluctant to write things down until fairly late in the communication process.

Such reluctance may be especially likely for people in collectivist cultures and who speak high-context languages. For these people, it is important to get consensus *before* a decision is broached, not after it is suggested. Resorting to writing before consensus is reached, therefore, can be very unnerving. For speakers of low-context languages, this may be less of a problem, as writing things down makes them even more explicit and more easy to understand and remember than speech; hence the frequent command, 'get it in writing'. Even for members of individualist cultures, however, written language can have legal and moral force, and writing may be filled with qualifications and hedges to get around the anticipated problems this medium can cause.

With the growing popularity of fax machines and e-mail, writing is used more and more often for more and more purposes, and some of the formal conventions around it are starting to break down or change. E-mail is especially informal. People often respond to e-mail spontaneously, with far less attention than they would give to a letter, not to mention a contract. This can lead to serious misunderstandings, even within a culture. For instance, a colleague sent a rather negative 'informal' job report by e-mail. He would not have done this in a letter, because he knew that the confidentially of his written report could not be guaranteed. To him, however, e-mail was like the telephone, and he wrote quite freely. Unfortunately, the e-mailed report was printed off and shown to the employee, which caused a lot of bad feeling all round. Our colleague felt that his confidence had been betrayed, but the person who printed off the report felt that, because it was written, it was just the same as a letter, and not confidential in that organisation.

This misunderstanding came about within a single culture—add the overlay of different cultural values and norms about writing versus speech, and the potential problems are compounded. At the same time, however, it is important to keep in mind that miscommunications such as this do happen every day *within* cultures. At present, as technology advances, social rules about how to use different communication media must change with it. Inevitably, people do not change at the same rate, and they end up disagreeing about what the new conventions, norms, and rules should be. For some people, incorrect spelling and grammar, as well as slapdash sentence construction, are quite appropriate on e-mail, as to them this medium is really 'written speech'. To others, however, writing is writing, whether it is e-mail, fax, letter, or contract, and they become incensed at 'bad' grammar or spelling. When people from another culture enter this arena of disagreement, they may feel as though they are in a no-win situation. If they make mistakes, some people hold them as accountable as they would be in a letter, but if they write carefully and formally, other colleagues think they lack spontaneity.

## Telephone—Almost Face-to-face Conversation

Telephones have been around for nearly a century now, and three generations of people have been born into societies (at least in urban areas) where the telephone is in common use. As a result, we have become accustomed to the telephone and have developed rules and conventions for handling this medium, just as we have long had them for face-to-face conversations. The difference between telephone and face-to-face communication, of course, is that non-vocal behaviour (gaze, facial expression, body movement, touch, and distance) are lost, and we must rely entirely on the communication we hear in the other person's voice and convey with our own. Fortunately, as we noted earlier, most or all of the verbal and non-verbal messages in face-to-face conversation can be conveyed by the voice alone. Evidence of this is provided by crisis lines and hot lines, where counsellors are able to conduct very sensitive conversations (even suicide prevention) successfully by telephone, using the voice alone.

We have developed special social rules for telephone conversations which help to make up for the things we cannot see. For example, in most cultures there are special ways of answering the telephone; in many languages, this involves a variant of the English word 'hello' (e.g., 'allo'). At work, many people in Western cultures answer the telephone by saying their name, something they would not do in face-to-face conversations, except perhaps as a way of introducing themselves to a stranger. Beyond this, listeners on the telephone typically interject a back-channel comment like 'mmhmm' or 'yes' on average every four seconds, much more frequently than they would do face-to-face. In this way, they make up for the lack of head nods and smiles which we use to indicate we are still listening when the other person can see us. Such rules go a long way to replacing non-vocal communication in most settings, but it is important to remember that, like all non-verbal communication, they are culture-specific.

In spite of the versatility of the voice as a communication medium, many people are uncomfortable using the telephone, especially for difficult or sensitive conversations, which they prefer to hold face-to-face. Part of the reason for this is the amount of attention people pay to the voice or to the body in understanding and decoding non-verbal communication. Noller (1984) found that, in the context of marriage, women tended to rely more on non-vocal communication, whereas men relied more on the voice. This may or may not be a good strategy, as Noller and Gallois

(1986) found that women produce facial expressions that convey Anglo-Celtic stereotypes about the expression of emotion more clearly than men do; for example, when they are trying to look happy, women smile, while men raise their eyebrows. How far these findings extend into the workplace is an open question, as many features of work—relative power, sex of the other person, importance of the task as against the relationship—are different from the home and family.

Even so, people who rely heavily on non-vocal communication and pay less attention to the voice are not likely to be happy telephone users. Neither are people who do not pay much attention to non-verbal behaviour at all, and who therefore need all the redundancy they can get in communication (remember that the non-verbal communication conveyed by the voice and by the non-vocal channels is highly redundant). In addition, in some situations it is difficult to pay attention to non-verbal behaviour, as the words or the context are disturbing in themselves. For example, if you are a boss who needs to tell an employee you are turning an unsatisfactory report or, even worse, sacking him, you may feel you must do this in person, simply because it is so difficult.

Intercultural communication is an area where many people feel more comfortable dealing face-to-face. One reason for this is that there is less redundancy in encounters where either or both parties are unfamiliar with the social rules for conversations. In these uncertain situations, people often feel a need to have all the information they can get, and the voice on its own leaves them in doubt about what the other person 'really' thinks. A second reason is that people are even less likely to know the specific rules for using the telephone in the other culture than the rules for face-to-face conversation. If they cannot interact in person because distance is too great, or there is not enough time, they may resort to writing on the grounds that at least they can get the words clear. This latter strategy is tempting, but anyone using it should keep in mind the differential impact of writing that we mentioned above.

## Choosing the Appropriate Communication Medium

At present, we do not know a great deal about people's reasons for choosing one type of communication over another. You might think that we would tend to choose written communication (fax, e-mail, letters) for more task-oriented communication, and the more personal forms of communication (face-to-face, telephone) where the relationship is more important or the communication is more difficult. Some recent research, however, indicates that this choice may not be so systematic (Kayany, Wotring & Forrest, 1996). In fact, convenience or familiarity with the technology may be more important considerations than the message being communicated. In particular, fax and e-mail are becoming more common in large multinational organisations because they are cheap and solve the problems of distance and time difference.

It is important at the present time not to let convenience or cost dictate all our choices of communication media. For instance, e-mail communication can be effective, and rules are developing to allow greater personal intimacy and informality on this medium, to the point that people sometimes meet their future spouses on the internet (Rintel & Pittam, 1997). Even so, it may be easier to work with a colleague through e-mail if there has been some personal contact, either through face-to-face meetings or telephone conversations. Such contact can flesh out the relationship enough that the colleagues trust their e-mail contacts. This may be even more true for faxes and letters, as these documents are permanent and confidentiality may not be protected using them. In general, the more the sources of communication in the relationship, the easier it is to detect misunderstandings and miscommunications, and to correct them.

## CONCLUSIONS

Most or all of our communication is governed by culture-specific social rules. These rules are tied to the values of a culture, and, like values, the rules may not be easily accessible to us. We may become aware of them only when they are broken. Strategies of politeness, in general, are used to repair rule violations as well as to prevent them, and these rules are especially important in difficult or sensitive communication situations. There is no cross-cultural dictionary of language or non-verbal behaviour, and we are even less likely to have one for social rules. Indeed, we may not even be able to write a book of rules for our own culture. Thus, there is an even greater need in intercultural encounters to

— slow down
— give the other person the benefit of the doubt
— be patient
— be extra polite
— wait and observe.

In other words, it is essential to pay extra attention to the communication process, even if this means it takes more time to get the task done. The time will turn out to be well spent.

Unfortunately, understanding the social rules of a situation, and using politeness and patience to repair misunderstanding, will not fix every intercultural communication problem. Sometimes, prejudice or hostility based on history make it difficult or impossible to communicate effectively with a person from another culture. Professional people, who often pride themselves on their open-mindedness and lack of prejudice, can find this aspect of intercultural communication especially hard to deal with. The next chapter takes up these issues, with the intention of adding some strategies to deal with them.

# 5

# SOCIAL IDENTITY, PREJUDICE, AND INTERCULTURAL COMMUNICATION

In this chapter, we take up the issues of prejudice and bias, and their impact on intercultural communication. It is clear that positive and negative feelings towards another person or group influence how we communicate with them. We will examine cases of misunderstanding that cannot be explained, at least not completely explained, by differences in social and cultural rules. In fact, to consider intercultural communication without considering prejudice—to assume that misunderstanding would disappear if we knew more about differences in cultural rules and practices—is far too optimistic. The rough-and-tumble of real encounters in society or the workplace is not so simple.

Sometimes, prejudice comes mainly from perceived differences in values or to stereotypes about others. Sometimes, however, it is the direct result of a long history of conflict between cultures. In 1995, during the fiftieth anniversary celebrations of the end of the Second World War, we heard an Australian veteran describe his bias against the Japanese as follows: 'Young Japanese people are fine, very intelligent, very considerate—and after all, none of this was their fault, they weren't even born. But I hate older Japanese—they're cruel and savage.' For him, the history of the war could never be erased, but he was willing to accommodate to present-day reality by drawing a sharp line across his view of the former enemy, based on age alone. In the following sections, we will look at the ways in which history, along with our values and our sense of cultural and group identity, influence every aspect of encounters with people from other cultures.

## INTERGROUP RELATIONS AND INTERCULTURAL INTERACTION

### History, Dominance, and Stereotypes

A number of years ago, we conducted a study of stereotypes about different cultural groups among young Australian adults (Callan & Gallois, 1983). We asked participants in the study to pick out of a list of traits, such as 'lazy', 'fun-loving', 'shrewd', 'passionate', and the like, the ones that best described a number of different cultural groups. They had clear, mostly positive, stereotypes about their own group, as well as for several other groups. For some groups, however, they told us that they had no stereotypes, as they did not know anyone from these groups. One of these groups, Turks, has an old history of conflict with Australians, and the Australian defeat at Gallipoli during the First World War is still much talked about. Despite their protests, these young adults, when asked to do the best they could, showed very clear, and negative, stereotypes about Turkish people. For still other groups (e.g., Albanians), they really did have no experience, and they even asked us for a hint about where these people lived. This time, no clear stereotypes about the group emerged. What this example reveals is that the history of relations between two groups alone is sometimes enough to produce stereotypes about people in those groups, even though people who hold the stereotypes are reluctant to admit it.

Before going further, we should define what we mean by 'stereotype'. This term is used in various ways by researchers and practitioners who study culture. Stereotypes in our usage refer to generalisations about groups of people. They may be positive or negative, but they are applied to most or all members of a group most or all of the time. Thus, they do not take much account of differences among individual people or across situations. Stereotypes are ubiquitous. It is impossible to avoid forming them about many groups, particularly when we are unfamiliar or uncertain of the situation (see Gudykunst, 1995; Tajfel & Turner, 1979). Stereotypes are useful to us, in that they help us to understand and predict the actions of others in our social world much more easily than would be possible without them. They give us guidelines about people and situations, reducing the demands on us of dealing with each person we encounter as a unique individual. On the other hand, they can make it harder to communicate with someone from another group, as we may communicate with the stereotype of the person's group, instead of the actual human being.

In thinking about stereotypes, we need to go one step further. We need to consider the process of categorising ourselves and others into groups in the first place. Again, such categories are ubiquitous. They extend to the physical world, and they help us to simplify various social judgements we make, especially about strangers (Brigham, 1977; Lippmann, 1922). In the 1960s, Henri Tajfel showed in a series of clever studies that the process of categorising people into social groups is just as ubiquitous (see Tajfel, 1979). He found that any cue at all, however trivial—eye colour, name, even an arbitrarily assigned label—was a sufficient basis for people to form groups, and to give biased judgements, some of which favoured the groups of which they themselves were members and disadvantaged other groups, even those formed using trivial criteria. In real life, of course, we have a wide range of ready-made group memberships—ethnic and cultural groups, sex, age, social class, religion, occupational group, hobby groups—into which we categorise ourselves and those around us. Once this process of self- and other-categorisation (Turner, 1987) has occurred, we make many other social judgements based on it. This is an important point—the initial judgements that formed the categorisation start to grow and become more and more generalised.

When there is a history of conflict, either short term or long term, such as existed for centuries between France and the German states, or where there is social inequality between two groups (for example, between Europeans and Africans in the United States and South Africa, or between Francophones and Anglophones in Canada), people tend to rationalise the situation using stereotypes. Where there is conflict, not surprisingly we tend to describe our own group in positive terms (patriotic, brave, successful, good) and members of the other group in very negative terms (lazy, sneaky, stupid, aggressive, savage). Where there is inequality, members of the dominant group are often described as more intelligent, beautiful, ambitious, powerful, and wealthy. Members of the disadvantaged group are seen as submissive, gentle, uneducated, friendly, and poor, by people in both groups (see Lambert et al., 1960). While each group has its own stereotype about itself and other groups, it is astonishing how often the words in the list above turn up, so much so that some authors have argued that it is possible to predict the history of relations between two groups from the stereotypes held by their members (see Ryan, Giles & Sebastian, 1982).

Within diglossic cultures, the two or more languages spoken may serve as a signal of such social inequality. For example, in regions colonised by foreigners, often the original inhabitants become diglossic in the colonial language and their native language or languages, using the former in public and official contexts and the latter at home and among themselves. The example in Chapter 2 which was taken from Paraguay (Rubin, 1970) is an example of this kind of diglossia.

Frequently, members of the politically dominant colonial group learn little or none of the native language. Instead, they rely on the multilingual skills of the natives to get around. This was the case in the main among the British in India and Africa during the colonial period, although there were individual exceptions. There are also cultural exceptions. For example, French colonists were more likely than British ones to learn the native languages of the countries where they were dominant, although they did not always do so either. Interestingly enough, members of dominated groups are rarely given credit for their language abilities by members of the dominant group. The same people who have learned two, three, or even more languages are still stereotyped as stupid, or criticised for their lack of perfect fluency by people who are completely monolingual themselves. The intercultural travellers of today should remember this, particularly those who can only speak one international language (English, French, Japanese) in the modern era of multiculturalism.

Of course, the relations between social groups or cultures do change. Economic relationships change, and a previously disadvantaged culture can, over a relatively short period of time, become richer and more powerful, as has happened in East Asia over the past 20 or 30 years. In addition, colonial empires come to an end, and inequality based on class or race is challenged. These large-scale factors have a strong impact on the stereotypes held by members of two groups about each other, as well as the way they communicate (cf. Taylor & McKirnan, 1984).

Four aspects of intergroup relations which are based in history or in the larger social structure appear to be especially important influences on intergroup communication (Giles & Johnson, 1987; Tajfel, 1979). The first of these is how *legitimate* people perceive the relations between the groups to be, and the second is how *stable* the situation is perceived to be. As long as most people think the inequality between two groups is appropriate, legitimate, and likely to continue (for whatever reason), relations between the groups tend to be low in hostility. Communication, usually in the dominant language or code, is relatively smooth, and stereotypes are positive or neutral. At some point, however, members of one group, usually the disadvantaged group, may begin to perceive the situation as illegitimate, and begin to push for change. Examples of this type of change can be found in consciousness-raising movements around the world. The stereotypes that members of the disadvantaged group hold of the dominant group become more negative, and those about their own group become more positive. At the same time, increased hostility among members of the dominant group towards outgroups increases, as people perceive changes as threatening the status quo which advantages them.

Changes in the third and fourth aspects also contribute to increased hostility and confrontation between groups, especially where there is a history of inequality. *Permeability* refers to the ease with which people can pass from one group to another. Groups where language and race are different tend to be relatively impermeable, particularly when they have a strongly held value of collectivism (Gallois et al., 1995). In other cases, permeability is so great that people must make a conscious effort to remain in their own group. An example of this today is in Northern Ireland, where the group distinction is based on religion, and language and ethnic group are the same. Finally, the *vitality* of the groups plays a role (Giles, Bourhis & Taylor, 1977). People who see their groups as strong in vitality and with a bright future may feel much greater pride than members of small minority groups whose vitality, in terms of numbers and political and economic power, is low. There are cases where vitality can have a paradoxical influence, however. For instance, people who believe their group is threatened by absorption into a permeable dominant group may work extra hard to preserve it (Cargile, Giles & Clément, in press; Sachdev et al., 1987). The movements to preserve and extend minority languages in Europe during the past 20 years are a good example of this. Languages like Welsh, Frisian, and Catalan, which were near extinction, have acquired a new lease of life as their speakers have reacted to this threat to vitality (see Cargile, Giles & Clément, in press).

## Social and Personal Identity

It is clear that large-scale social forces have an influence on stereotypes, prejudice, and bias between people from different cultures and groups, and that the languages spoken in a multicultural community are a reflection of intergroup relations. But how do these sociostructural factors affect communication between professionals, or between professionals and their clients, across cultures? How, in other words, does the social and historical situation influence communication between individuals? To explain this, we will use a theory of identity which has been extremely influential in communication, *social identity theory* (Tajfel, 1979; Tajfel & Turner, 1979; Turner, 1987). A central tenet of this theory is to describe 'the group in the individual' (Hogg & Abrams, 1988, p. 17).

If you were asked to describe yourself in five words or short phrases, what would you say? The answer to this question gives some insight into your self-concept, or your image of your own essential characteristics. In fact, the answer is likely to depend on who asks the question, and in what circumstances. Let us use the example of a friend of ours, who we will call Mark Edwards. Mark is a school counsellor in a large mixed-sex high school. When a close friend asked him to describe himself, he said something like this, 'I am a hard-working person, enjoy sport, have a good sense of humour, am a family man, and am creative.' These phrases all serve to pick Mark out from his friends, people who come from the same place and do similar work—he is the creative, witty one who likes sport. In addition, all the phrases are fairly positive, which may help Mark's sense of self-esteem or self-worth. Because all these phrases are linked to Mark as an individual and in interpersonal relationships (his family in the example), and they distinguish him from similar people, they can be said to form part of his *personal identity*—his sense of himself as an individual, based on interpersonal comparisons with people in his own social groups (Tajfel & Turner, 1979).

Imagine another context—Mark and his colleagues are criticised by a number of parents of students at his school, for being insensitive to the social and cultural needs of girls from a minority ethnic group in the community. The staff at the school are angry about this. They feel they have done everything they can to promote multiculturalism and sensitivity to other cultures. If he were thinking about this situation, Mark might describe himself something like this, 'I'm a school counsellor, a helping professional, a sensitive person, an Australian, and a good father.' Only one characteristic has been retained from the first list. This time, Mark describes himself in much more group-related terms, and ones which contrast his group directly with the parents who have made the complaints—he is a professional (they are not), he is Australian (they have raised the issue of culture), he is a good father (the complaints are about daughters), and so forth. Once again, notice that all the characteristics are positive,—which may help to enhance Mark's self-esteem by creating a positive image of his occupational group and his national group as against the outgroup in this situation. This time, the traits can be said to form part of Mark's *social identity* (Tajfel & Turner, 1979).

Which one of these descriptions picks out the real Mark Edwards? Both of them do, but in different ways. All of us have individual characteristics that we think of as our personality or our unique personal identity—these are the things that distinguish us from others, but which we may also use to find our friends. At the same time, we belong to a number of groups, and we think of these groups in terms of characteristics that distinguish them from other relevant groups—our social identity. Both personal and social identity help to reduce uncertainty, by providing a stable characterisation of us as individuals and as group members. In addition, they help to provide a positive self-image for us.

Personal and social identity are not always at the forefront of our minds. Which one is salient at any particular moment depends upon the situation. When we are among members of our ingroups, or communicating in a friendly, cooperative situation as individuals, personal identity is more likely to be salient (see Hogg & Abrams, 1988). Thus, we tend to emphasise the individual differences between ourselves and others, as well as between other people—we see the people around us as distinctive individuals, and we communicate with them as individuals. On the other hand, when the situation is threatening, or when there is competition for scarce resources, rivalry, or hostility between groups, social identity is more likely to be salient. In these kinds of situations, we tend to minimise the individual differences between people and exaggerate the differences between our group and other groups. We communicate with others either as members of our ingroups or as outgroup members, but in both cases as group members rather than as individuals. We are very likely to rely on stereotypes to guide our behaviour, rather than deal with the idiosyncratic features of the people in the situation (see Oakes, Haslam & Turner, 1994; Turner, 1987).

Even though the characteristics in our personal and social identities may remain fairly constant over time, their salience changes in a very fluid way. For example, in a business environment a manager may see herself as cooperative and careful towards her own work group, and she may see her subordinates in terms of individual characteristics (one is a hard worker, another is brilliant but lazy, and so forth). When she is dealing with a union representative, however, her social identity as a manager is much more salient. She sees herself as a tough negotiator who will not give in to his unreasonable demands. Later in the cafeteria, she thinks of the same shop steward in his role as a fellow parent, as she talks with him about a problem with the school their children both attend. She may even make an exception of him in his role as a shop steward, thinking to herself, 'a lot of union reps are stupidly stubborn, but this one is a bit different'. Even later, when the company is threatened by a hostile takeover from a foreign multinational, she thinks of both herself and the union representative as rational people who must fight this attack by outsiders. Her salient social identity changes from situation to situation, and her impression of the shop steward changes along with it.

Does this mean that the manager's impression of union representatives, or of the foreign company, are also very fluid? Not really—as the context changes, different group memberships, and the identities that go with them, are invoked, but the stereotypes that attach to each identity and each group remain much the same. In fact, because she has made an exception of this union representative, her judgement of union representatives in general may be even less likely to change—she has taken him explicitly out of one identity and communicated with him in terms of another (Hewstone & Brown, 1986).

## SOCIAL IDENTITY AND INTERCULTURAL COMMUNICATION

When we interact with people from another culture, our social identity is likely to be salient from the moment we see that they look different, and from the first word we hear of their language or accented speech. In fact, many studies have shown that the language and accent of a speaker alone are enough to produce very different judgements of the speaker's characteristics (see Giles & Coupland, 1991; Ryan & Giles, 1982, for reviews). Intercultural communication is a form of intergroup communication. It has much in common with communication across other group memberships—sex, social class, and so forth. In part, we are communicating to our stereotypes about the group, rather than to the real individuals. This aspect of social identity is illustrated well by the businessman who says, 'The Japanese are so hard to deal with—they are inscrutable, they never let you know where you stand.' As we pointed out in earlier chapters, statements like these come about partly because of differences in values: in this case, the sharp and impermeable group boundaries that tend to characterise collectivist cultures. They may also stem from different social rules: in this case, the appropriateness of not revealing one's true intentions in business transactions. But in this example, they also come from the businessman's stereotypes of the Japanese, based on the history of his culture's relations with Japan and on previous experiences he has had. In other words, the Japanese person he is dealing with may be fairly straightforward and honest with him, but the businessman does not notice—he sees the stereotype rather than the individual person.

Stereotypes can influence our judgement so strongly that they can obscure behaviour that is completely contrary to them. For example, a colleague we know was teaching a group of Thai students in a postgraduate course. These people were new to the country, unfamiliar with the academic environment, and very anxious to do well. In fact, their future depended on it. Our colleague had a very strong stereotype of Thais as gentle and non-aggressive people, and she went out of her way to encourage these students to participate in class. A few weeks into the semester, she began to receive complaints from the other students that two of the Thai students were dominating the discussion, and the other students could not get a word in. She did not take these complaints very seriously, since she was sure the Thai students were too quiet, not too assertive in discussion. Some time later, the other students were so incensed that they brought up the complaints in class. This caused great embarrassment to the Thai students, who had got the impression from their teacher that they should participate as much as possible—after all, she kept asking them to talk! Our colleague's stereotypes had got in the way. She had not been able to make an accurate judgement about the amount these particular students were participating, and thus to prevent the problem from becoming so serious.

## Multiple Group Memberships

Intercultural encounters, of course, do not occur in a social void. The people who meet across cultures do so for a reason, usually one connected with their work. This means they deal with each other in terms of their occupational as well as their cultural identities. In addition, they have a gender, an age, and a social class which may also influence their behaviour. Beyond their group memberships, they have individual characteristics that are important to communication. They may, for example, be extroverted and ready to communicate with anyone; they may be very task-oriented, and not interested in small talk. Finally, the situation may be formal or informal, threatening or comfortable, and the task itself may be difficult or easy to explain. These factors interact with each other in determining how any intercultural communication proceeds. This means that culture may not be the most important social identity in an intergroup interaction. Sex, age, or occupation may be much more salient. In addition, personality factors and individual values and beliefs may change an intercultural encounter very greatly (Pittam & Gallois, 1996).

A study we have conducted over the past few years will illustrate the importance of multiple group memberships on intercultural communication (Jones et al., 1995). We have been interested in communication between Australians and Chinese overseas students from several countries in Southeast Asia, especially when the overseas students are very fluent speakers of English. With these people, we have been able to examine communication problems and issues that are not to do with language fluency. Thus, we have observed Chinese students communicating with Australian students and with Australian members of the academic staff about their work as students.

The results of this research reveal one overwhelming thing—that occupational role (staff member or student) is more important than cultural group or gender in determining how these people communicate with each other. For example, both Australian and Chinese students conversing with other students were more equal in participation than when a staff member was involved: the staff member tended to direct the discussion more than the student. Male and female staff members did this in different ways—the men tended to tell stories about their own life as students and to give advice, while the women tended to ask questions and encourage the students to talk about themselves. Nevertheless, in both cases, the staff members determined most of what was talked about and how. In addition, communication by male and female students was more similar when they talked to staff members than when they talked to other students, an indication that the staff–student conversations were more strongly governed by social rules about formality, register, and the like.

This is not to say that there were no differences based on the cultural group of the students; there were. Rather, these differences paled in comparison to the differences based on occupational role. It is important to remember this in any intercultural encounter: do not assume that culture will always be the dominant factor governing how things will go. In addition, not everyone from the same culture acts the same, and the situation makes a difference too. We will discuss differences based on occupational and organisational role in more detail in the next chapter.

## Communication Accommodation and Intercultural Interactions

In the past two chapters, we have introduced a large number of factors that can and do influence intercultural communication. In this section, we will try to bring them together. The first question is: *Who must adapt to whom?* In an intercultural interaction, whose responsibility is it to understand the communication practices and rules of the other?

Some writers have argued that this task falls mainly on the sojourner—when in Rome, do as the Romans do. In some cases, this is certainly true. For example, students doing a degree in a foreign country, business people who are abroad for a short period, and even some immigrants, must conform to the host culture, as they are usually not sufficiently numerous or powerful to induce the host culture to conform to them (see Kim, 1988, 1995). They learn to adapt by reading and watching the mass media in the new culture, as this is a way of observing the culture and learning communication practices without much chance of making a mistake. In addition, the more they interact with people in the host culture, the more quickly and successfully they adapt to it. As we have pointed out in previous chapters, members of their home culture can sometimes make it hard for them to adapt, by urging them to cling to the old ways. In addition, they may get away with continuing in their original communication practices if their group is powerful enough. For example, if their company has set up a subsidiary in the host culture, they may not need to learn the host language, but this situation is likely to cause resentment and bias towards them.

In fact, the kind of situation where only one person needs to adapt, and where adaptation proceeds fairly easily, is relatively uncommon, even among short-term visitors to a culture. This is because the relations between the groups once again have an influence. For example, tourists in a foreign country are there for only a brief moment, and one would think that they would need to adapt to the host culture. They are not motivated to do this, however—they are there to have a good time (Pearce, 1982). People in the host culture may feel they are obliged to adapt to the tourists, because they need the business, and so most of the adaptation may go the other way. The same thing may apply in the case of foreign students. These people are in a culture for a longer period, but they are paying tuition fees that are important to their new universities. In this case, people on both sides may feel they are being forced to adapt to each other. Even in the case of

immigrants, if the group is large and vital enough it m[...]
pressure on the host culture to recognise its unique chara[...]
teristics, its language, and so forth (see Giles & Coupland,
1991). Transactions across cultures are filled with complexity,
and the responsibility for adapting is yet another one.

A more complex model seems to be necessary to capture the
complications of adaptation. One such model is *communication
accommodation theory* (Gallois et al., 1995; Giles & Coupland,
1991). Communication accommodation theory starts from the
assumption that, in any intercultural interaction, people are
motivated to communicate with each other either in more
interpersonal terms (i.e., talk to each other as individuals, in
terms of their personal identity) or in more intergroup terms
(i.e., talk to each other as group members, in terms of social
identity). Which of these motives they have depends on all the
factors we mentioned above. When the two groups have a
history of rivalry or inequality, and especially when the relations between the groups are in a state of flux, people are
more likely to interact in more intergroup ways. For example,
at the present time British people are likely to be more conscious of their British identity as they communicate with
French or German people, because their place in the European
Union is being negotiated. On the other hand, when a new
social identity emerges that includes both groups, communication is likely to be more interpersonal. Thus, more black and
white South Africans at the present moment may treat each
other as individuals than happened a few years ago, when
apartheid was still in force.

Secondly, the salient social and personal identities of the
people in the interaction crucially influence how they interact,
and in particular how motivated they are to treat each other as
individuals. If their *social* identities are salient, as they are
likely to be in a very formal or threatening situation, they may
interact with each other in terms of stereotypes. If things are
going well and they are comfortable in the situation, on the
other hand, they are more likely to perceive each other's

individual traits, as well as acting more in terms of their personal identity. In addition, when their social identities are salient, they are less likely to be tolerant of mistakes or violations of their social rules by people from another culture—they may be more ready to say, 'See—I told you they were like that—this proves it!'

Finally, as we noted earlier, the situation itself has a role to play here. The rules that apply in the situation put constraints and limits on how we can behave. For example, in a very formal situation, we may be obliged by the rules to interact with polite distance, no matter what we want to do. This can be very frustrating when we wish to behave more interpersonally, but it can also take the heat out of interactions that otherwise would be very intergroup. On the other hand, we may find ways even in very formal and rule-governed situations to express our view of the other person or the person's cultural group. Furthermore, unfamiliar situations are stressful in themselves, and we may react to them by behaving in a more intergroup way. Intercultural travellers should take account of this, and should not try to do too much during their first days in a new cultural environment, until they have got over the worst of the stress of unfamiliarity (not to mention jet lag).

## Accommodative Communication: Convergence and Divergence

One major way we show whether we are thinking about the other people in an encounter as individuals or as group members is in how we adapt our speech, language, and non-verbal communication to theirs. If we see the interaction mainly in interpersonal terms, or if we wish to show our liking and approval for the other group's culture, we may change our language, accent, or other behaviour to be more like theirs; this is called *convergence* (Giles & Coupland, 1991). On the other hand, we can show our dislike or disapproval for the other group's culture through *divergence*.

The process of convergence happens frequently in conversations with friends, family, or close colleagues. Think of the case of a teenager who has left home to go to university in another town (or another country). When the child telephones home, his accent seems changed to the family. The child has converged to the new environment, and has 'picked up' the way his fellow students speak. During the conversation, however, his accent is likely to revert to one more like his family's—so much so that his room-mates may remark on his change to 'down home' speech. Some people are more prone to this kind of convergence than others, just as some people have a better ear for accents in foreign languages. For many of us, convergence happens without our being aware of it until it is pointed out to us.

In intercultural encounters, the same process is likely to occur if we like the other person. We may suddenly find ourselves gesturing in the same way, using the same words, and sounding more like the other person in accent. If we have the ability, we may go further and switch into the other person's language if it is different from our own. On the other hand, if we disapprove of the other person or the person's culture, we may emphasise differences between our behaviours. For example, we may maintain our own accent and speech patterns and not move at all towards the other person's. We may even exaggerate our accent to emphasise the difference, or simply refuse to speak the other person's language even though we know how. This can sometimes lead to strange situations, as the following example shows.

The decade of the 1960s was a time of rising cultural and ethnic consciousness in Belgium, particularly among Flemish speakers. These people had been politically dominated for many centuries, first by the Spanish, then the Dutch, and finally by French-speaking Walloons. They were starting to demand what they considered to be appropriate recognition of their own language in this officially bilingual country. Flemish had, during the years after the Second

World War, undergone a standardisation process to produce a standard Flemish grammar, spelling, and vocabulary; such standardisation is an important process in producing a more positive social identity (see Ryan & Giles, 1982). As part of this process, standard Flemish eliminated French words and spellings to a much greater extent than Dutch, the version of the language spoken in the Netherlands. In 1968, things were beginning to come to a head, with the rise of a Flemish party, the Volksunie. Eventually, the country would be divided into a federation with Flemish speaking and French-speaking regions, and only the capital, Brussels, would remain bilingual. At the time, however, things had not yet gone this far.

Into the middle of this rather tense language situation came the revolutionary student movements that paralysed France and brought upset to a number of other countries, including Belgium. For a period, universities in Brussels were occupied by left-wing student groups, who had a strong agenda and who were highly motivated to cooperate with each other. But what language should they speak? If they chose French, Flemish students might be offended (as, later, Bourhis et al., 1979, found they were). If they chose Flemish, French-speaking students might feel threatened. So, often, they chose English, a neutral language in that context which none of them objected to, but which none of them spoke very well. The rest of the time, one side or the other converged. The overarching social identity of student activist was strong enough to counteract the desire to diverge based on their ethnic identity, for a time at least.

People who are not familiar with cultural conflicts like this can find them difficult to understand. To an outsider, it may seem silly or obstinate for one person to refuse to speak another's language, even though the first person is perfectly capable of doing so. It is important to remember, however, that language, accent, and non-verbal behaviour operate as key markers of identity. Thus, it is *identity as signalled by language and communication*, that is seen to be under threat and that the person insists on emphasising. When we encounter this kind of divergence—a patient, for example, who steadfastly refuses to accommodate to a doctor's communication by answering the doctor's questions—it is essential to consider the possibility that the patient's identity is threatened by the doctor, the situation, or the whole cultural environment. What we are seeing is not so much a clash of communication as a clash of identities.

How should we handle this kind of situation, where one person diverges and refuses to change? Beyond the guidelines we have already suggested, the most important thing is to be aware of what is going on. First, remember that this is not just a communication issue—an important social identity is at stake. Secondly, keep in mind that the other person may or may not be aware of what is happening—indeed, sometimes people think they are converging when to others they seem to be diverging. Thirdly, be aware that you may be doing the same thing yourself—the other person may be reacting to your own divergence. It may be possible, by treating the person more as an individual and by converging yourself, to bring the interaction to a friendlier level.

## CONCLUSIONS

This chapter has concentrated on examining the reasons for misunderstanding and hostility between people in different cultures that cannot be easily explained in terms of different rules or even different values. To analyse such miscommunications, we must look further—to the economic, social, and historical relations between cultures. There may be times when absolutely nothing will help to make communication friendlier or more interpersonal, but we believe that these occasions are relatively rare. Most of the time, we can minimise the impact of prejudice by understanding how it works, and by slowing down enough to get beyond our own stereotypes and to communicate with the people we meet *as individuals.* It is important to keep several things in mind:

1. The history of relations between two groups is an important influence on communication between their members.
2. The process of categorising people into groups and forming stereotypes about them is an inescapable fact of social life.
3. When there is conflict, rivalry, or threat between two groups, people communicate to the other group as a whole, rather than to the individuals in it.
4. Making your own speech style more like that of people in another culture, or speaking in their language, is an important signal that you like them and approve of their culture.

# 6

# INTERCULTURAL COMMUNICATION WITHIN ORGANISATIONS

In the preceding chapters, we have looked at various aspects of intercultural communication, introducing a number of principles as well as some concrete guidelines for professional practice. We have emphasised two main contributors to misunderstanding when people communicate between cultures. The first is the *social and cultural rules* operating in the situation, and the second is the *intergroup relations* between the cultures, including the ways these relations affect social identity and prejudice. For the rest of the book, we will look at the way these principles operate in different contexts, and we will examine the special features and problems in each context. This chapter deals with the heart of organisational life—communicating with job applicants, colleagues, subordinates, and superiors. As we have pointed out in earlier chapters, the same things that cause communication problems within a culture often appear when more than one culture is involved. When more than one culture is involved, however, these problems tend to be perceived as due to cultural differences, rather than to other factors like role, status, and personality. We begin with the job selection process, including job applications and interviews.

## INTERCULTURAL COMMUNICATION AND THE SELECTION PROCESS

## Job Applications

Imagine the following situation. Joe Turner is a personnel officer looking at applicants for a senior position in a large public sector organisation. The organisation deals with people inside and outside the country, as well as being involved with several different ethnic client groups in the country. As a result, the organisation has a vigorous equal opportunity policy in hiring. Joe has a policy of going out of his way to solicit applications from people in the main ethnic and national groups the organisation deals with. In the case of this job, he has tried to encourage Indians to apply. The position is very attractive, and a large number of applications have been received. Joe is now at the point of shortlisting for interview, and he is worried.

In looking at the applications, Joe has noticed that the native-born Anglo applicants in this English-speaking country have submitted concise résumés, detailing their work histories, qualifications, and special skills, as well as listing the names of several referees. Many of the Indian applicants, however, have produced very brief résumés (to Joe, they seem cryptic), but have included all their diplomas and certificates, as well as testimonial references. This has really put Joe off—why have these people done so little work on their résumés? And why are they including such irrelevant information? He is stuck, because he would prefer to shortlist only Anglo applicants, as they seem much better qualified for the work, but the organisation will not appreciate this apparent flouting of the equal opportunity policy.

What is going on in this example? Are the Anglo applicants really better qualified, or is culture playing a hidden role? Do the Indian applicants have problems with written English, so that they are producing short and cryptic résumés, or is this yet another example of different cultural rules? As you have no doubt already guessed, the most likely explanation for the problem is the last one. The rules for writing job applications are subtle and difficult in all cultures, as this is a specialised situation that most people encounter only a handful of times in their working lives. Even professional people, who are usually more sensitive to the requirements of applying for new positions, and who may go through this process more frequently than other people, often find putting together a résumé or curriculum vitae a trying task. One reason is that the activity is so rule-bound. In English-speaking countries, this process has become so specialised that placement agencies and others give formal classes on preparing applications. In Indian culture, the situation is very similar, but the rules are different. Different parts of the person's history, in particular clear evidence of all relevant qualifications, take on extra importance, and presenting a concise but clear picture of the whole application is relatively less important. The same issue applies in European countries and other parts of Asia—in other words, each country, or rather each employment community, has its own rules for application forms.

Unfortunately, even in countries where low-context languages are spoken, these rules are rarely communicated explicitly in job advertisements. Instead, at best, the bare bones of the job description and the selection criteria are given. It should be no surprise that people interpret these brief instructions in terms of their own rules. In hindsight, Joe Turner may have avoided some difficulties by giving more complete instructions for how to apply, since he wanted to receive many good applications from non-Anglo people. While doing this would certainly have helped, however, it would probably not have solved the problem completely. This is because cultural rules are usually sufficiently ingrained to override even fairly detailed instructions. In any case, if he realises that the problem is caused by different rules rather than sloppiness or inadequate qualifications, he may be less inclined to blame the applicants for not getting their applications 'right'.

What is Joe to do now, however? He is confronted with a set of applications that may not give a true picture of how good the applicants are. He wants to be unbiased in making the decision about who to shortlist, but the applications from English-speaking applicants look better no matter how hard he tries to remember the role of social and cultural rules. In other words, Joe's own rules keep getting in the way of his ability to decide among the applicants based on their actual qualifications. First, he must be aware of what is happening. He needs to avoid the great temptation to blame the applicants for their 'bad' applications. Then, he needs to allow for a number of possible reasons for the form of the applications, and in particular for the operation of different rules. This does not mean that Joe has to become familiar with the rules for job applications in every culture he deals with; as we have pointed out already, this is likely to be an impossible task. Even so, as he becomes more experienced with applications from people from a specific culture, he will get some sense of their special features. This familiarity may help him decide among different applicants, just as he does with applicants from his own culture.

In the meantime, he has little option but to put extra time into shortlisting, so that he can read beyond the form of the applications to see the real academic and work history. For example, he may decide to talk to referees earlier in the process than he normally would, to gain an additional source of information about each applicant. Beyond this, he may need to make up a table to recast all the applications in terms of the specific selection criteria for the job. If he does this, he will have eliminated some of the impact of the application format. Again, experience is a good teacher here, and personnel officers need to recognise the need for extra time and attention—perhaps even the need for a secretary who can recast the applications before they are judged. This process will help to ensure fairness, which is important for a member of an individualist culture like Joe. On the other hand, it will be more costly in time and money than the organisation's normal procedures, which may clash with the organisational value placed on efficiency.

Joe may find himself being forced to choose among several conflicting values. He needs to have a clear idea of which values are most important to him and to the organisation, in the light of the value placed on equality and non-discrimination in the culture as a whole. Professional and business organisations in many countries often have not achieved a very good record in hiring members of minority cultural groups (or sub-cultural groups and women). Subtle factors like the format of the applications are often implicated. So it may well be in the organisation's interest for Joe to take extra time over the shortlisting process, even though it is costly. In addition, if this experience is successful, the organisation may have a better idea of how to advertise the next job so that the form of the applications received are more similar.

## Job Interviews

Let us continue with the case of Joe Turner, who has succeeded in producing a short list with both Anglo and Indian applicants. To do this, he has gone to some effort in reading the applications, and he has also shortlisted a larger than usual number of people. He calls together a panel of three people, including the manager of the unit where the successful applicant will work and the organisation's equal employment opportunity officer. They set up an interview schedule, and the next part of the process gets under way. Once again, Joe and the rest of the panel are confronted with the difficulties of navigating different, and sometimes contradictory, social rules.

The Anglo applicants present with a great deal of initiative. Most of them are very positive in describing themselves and their qualifications, as well as their desire to do this job and to contribute their special skills to the organisation. Their positive and assertive behaviour comes across very well, as research results from many studies (e.g., Gallois, Callan & McKenzie Palmer, 1992) would predict. The Indian applicants, however, are more diffident. They wait to be asked. They give answers that seem rather equivocal and almost too polite. They are very positive, smiling a lot and agreeing, but they do not seem very assertive. Their accent in English makes the unit manager think they are not very fluent in the language. As they did in their written applications, they emphasise their diplomas and qualifications, and are very modest about their skills and the individual contribution they can make to the organisation. They give an impression of being less independent to the members of the panel who are Anglo, and less able to take on the responsibilities of this professional position.

It seems clear to the panel that the Anglo applicants are much better suited to the job. Joe even wonders why he went to all the trouble with the shortlisting process. The interviews seem to 'prove' that the native-born applicants are superior. In fact, however, the same process is operating in the interviews as in the written applications: the Anglo and Indian applicants are following different rules. This time, the communication patterns can be traced to the individualist values of Anglo-Celtic cultures and the more collectivist orientation of Indian culture. The Anglo applicants set out to show themselves off to good advantage, but in a positive assertive manner, and they emphasise the worth of their individual contribution. This is what their culture encourages them to do. The Indian applicants, in following their culture's rules, emphasise their worth in terms of other people's opinions of them—for example, their diplomas and certificates, which prove they are well-credentialled—and they work to show that they can fit into the organisation's hierarchy and get along in it without difficulty, by being polite and not taking issue with what is said to them.

The interview panel Joe has set up is composed of well-qualified people, but all of them are Anglo and none of them has much experience with Indian culture. The rules about communication in interviews are, if anything, even more strict and ingrained than the rules about writing job applications. In fact, personnel officers believe that they can predict the suitability of an applicant from the person's interview performance (see Ramsay, Gallois & Callan, in press), even though research evidence suggests that this may not be true. Factors like accent have an important impact on hiring decisions (Ball et al., 1984; Seggie, Fulmizi & Stewart, 1982; Willemyns et al., 1997). All the panellists, therefore, are likely to fall into the trap of thinking that their style of communication is good communication, or the 'right' way to communicate in this organisation. Thus, they may conclude that even though the Indian applicants are well qualified and possess the necessary skills for the job, they will not perform as well as the Anglos. Even the equal employment opportunity officer, who is responsible for making sure there is no discrimination in hiring, may yield to this conclusion if she is not sensitive to the influence of cultural rules on verbal and non-verbal communication in contexts like interviews.

Someone must be hired, however, so how should the panel decide? As always, they need first to be aware of what is going on: their own social rules are playing an important role in their impressions of the applicants, and so is their social identity. Up to now, they have not made much attempt to distinguish among individual applicants, as the really salient thing has been their cultural group and their different behaviour in the interview. It could be useful at this point to rank the applicants separately by cultural group. Once they are in a position to compare the very best Anglo and Indian applicants, some of their concerns about presentation may disappear, since the best applicants are likely to be more flexible and sensitive to the situation. If they consider the clients of the organisation, they need a culturally sensitive professional. Indeed, this could be an essential selection criterion, and they need to take it seriously.

The panel also should consider the specifics of the job very carefully. Who will the successful applicant be working with?

It is easy to go wrong if the client group is not taken account of, and this is harder to do when the clients come from another culture. For example, we were on a selection committee recently where a teacher was being hired. In this school, students had frequently complained that they could not understand the foreign teachers. Whether this was accurate or not, the panel were very concerned to select an applicant whose spoken language was crystal clear and easy to follow. This did not mean that only native speakers were shortlisted, but all speakers were judged on clarity of speech, something that may not have been done if the students' wishes had not been considered. On the other hand, we know of an American company that was operating in Japan. The selection committees had a practice of hiring American managers to work in the Tokyo office. They tended to hire people with the qualities Americans desire in managers—assertiveness, gregariousness, initiative, plain speech, and a go-ahead approach. These people would have performed well in the United States, but they were badly out of touch with their Japanese clients and co-workers, who would have preferred a quiet American team player.

In the case of Joe Turner's organisation and the position in question, the successful person will be dealing mainly with Indian clients. Thus, the panel may once again have to pause before following their intuitions about who to hire. They may need to take extra advice from referees, and it may be useful to give the best applicants a brief trial working with real clients. This job sample may change their impressions greatly. Once again, this process is more costly than relying on the interview alone. The cost is worth paying, however, if the applicant is better able to deal with the client group.

## COMMUNICATING WITH SUBORDINATES, SUPERVISORS, AND COLLEAGUES

Most of working life involves interactions with people we know—our own colleagues, subordinates, and bosses—rather than making predictions about the future performance of job applicants. In these kinds of interactions, we have plenty of opportunity to judge people as individuals, and to see the individual characteristics and behaviour of those around us. Thus, we are likely to think that culture will matter less. We should be able to get beyond our stereotypes about other cultures and the different rules used by people in them and see the real traits of others at work. In some ways, this is true. Certainly, we are more likely to pin our judgements onto the behaviour of individual people. Even so, as the promotion and job turnover rates in many organisations indicate, social identity and social rules still play an important role in judgements about others. We will discuss several key and sensitive areas where these factors tend to have an especially large impact, with a view to locating ways to minimise their influence.

# Communicating about Performance: Managing Downwards

### Giving instructions and information: the case of Joan Wilson

Consider the following exchange between a supervisor, Joan Wilson, and her employee, Louise Delhaye, who work in a multinational legal firm:

JOAN: Louise, I need the Sullivan case to be gone through carefully, to make sure the financial details and the timetabling are right, and that nothing stands out as a glaring omission—can you see to it?

LOUISE: Yes, Joan.

JOAN: And I need it for next week, to take to the full meeting on Tuesday—is that okay?

LOUISE: Fine, Joan.

JOAN: If you have any problems or need anything, please let me know—this is really important.

LOUISE: Of course Joan.

JOAN: Any worries at this stage?

LOUISE: No, don't worry about anything, Joan.

JOAN: Thanks, Louise, I knew you could do it.

This is the kind of exchange that occurs every day in all sorts of organisations and that gives subordinates nightmares. Looked at carefully, every line of Joan's instructions leaves ambiguity and the possibility for miscommunication. In the first line, what does Joan mean by 'glaring omissions'? How detailed are the details? In her second line, is she saying she needs the report by Tuesday or by Monday, or perhaps even by Friday, so she can prepare for the meeting over the week-end? And so forth. Joan is likely to think she was clear, and also that she gave plenty of opportunity for Louise to ask questions or to check later. In one sense she has done this, but it would be easy to forgive Louise for thinking her supervisor was not really interested in giving more information—her message emphasises the importance of the job, and her desire for Louise to take the initiative and do it.

Even if Joan and Louise come from the same culture, Joan is likely to be disappointed in Louise's performance, because she has taken little account of the realities of the power structure. It is a basic feature of organisational life that when supervisors and subordinates communicate, there is pressure on subordinates to agree, to be seen to be doing the right thing, and to present themselves well (see Shockley-Zalabak, 1991; Sias & Jablin, 1995). Thus, it is in Joan's, or any supervisor's, interest, to make sure that her instructions are clearly understood and agreed to, and that Louise really does feel free to get help if she needs it later. Joan can do this by asking checking questions, such as 'Are there any financial details that you're not sure about?' She can also ask Louise to paraphrase, 'What do you think the most likely omissions are?'; ask for progress reports, 'Tomorrow, can you give me an outline of how far you have got and any problems?'; or give specific times when Louise can find her to ask questions, 'I'll be in every afternoon, so please check with me if you need anything at all.' These strategies are not a panacea—the possibility for misunderstanding is still there—but they do make it easier for Louise to ask for help later if she realises she has not understood everything.

If Louise does get something wrong, Joan is likely to blame her for not paying enough attention, or not working hard enough, or not being skilled enough—or maybe, if she is especially sensitive, she may blame herself for not being clear enough. In other words, she will explain the mistake in personal or interpersonal terms. It may not come to this—Louise may realise that she must get this job right, and take the risk of asking questions, or she may find another experienced employee to ask, so that she does not risk displeasing Joan. If she does this, any misunderstandings may be fixed before they cause problems, and both Joan and Louise will forget the incident and remember only that the job was done well. This is likely to reinforce the feeling on both their parts that they have communicated well. In short, when things go right we tend to take credit for communicating well, and when things go wrong we look for someone else to blame.

Within cultures, this is the stuff of thousands of organisational training programmes. When we add the extra ingredient of intercultural communication, the possibilities for miscommunication are multiplied. Consider the exchange above again, and imagine that Louise comes from a collectivist culture that uses high-context language, while Joan comes from an individualist culture that employs low-context language. In this case, Joan is likely to think she has been very specific and clear, by giving examples, and that Louise should take the initiative and ask questions if she does not understand. For Louise, however, it is important to preserve harmony and not to disagree with her supervisor, who says she is confident that Louise will do a good job. In any case, it is the supervisor's role to make sure the job is done properly and to take responsibility for it in the name of the work group, so Joan will make sure the report is right before she takes it to the meeting. In her culture, there is no need to say this, it is assumed.

In this intercultural case, when things go wrong, Joan and Louise are likely to blame each other, particularly as there is a fundamental disagreement about the roles of each of them, and this issue has not been broached. Beyond this, however, they may go on to blame each other's culture. Joan may think something like, 'Those people never will take any initiative, no matter what you tell them,' while Louise may believe that 'People in Joan's culture are just power abusers—they never take responsibility for anything.' Notice that, in these statements, the actions of one person have been generalised to the whole culture ('those people') and the actions have been described in terms of enduring characteristics ('never will take responsibility'; see Semin & Fiedler, 1992). Because social identity is salient in this kind of encounter, the damage done by miscommunication is even greater than it is within a single culture—and it is bad enough there.

How can Joan fix this problem? There is no simple solution, but, as always, being aware of the possibility of miscommunication is a big step towards avoiding it and repairing it when it does occur. A key part of awareness is to realise that miscommunication is normal in organisational life. Fortunately, most miscommunications are small and easily repaired, so that at worst they are a source of minor irritation. Even so, it is important to remember that the bad mistakes are not the only ones. Indeed, supervisors who expect to be at least partially misunderstood, rather than understood, are likely to be much more careful in their communication.

A second step in avoiding or repairing miscommunication is to check and re-check for understanding. This process can be passive; that is, supervisors can ask questions that open up opportunities to check for understanding. It should also be active, however, especially where subordinates come from cultures with rules or values against disagreeing in public or questioning the actions of superiors. The more active process of checking includes asking subordinates to paraphrase instructions, asking for progress reports, and making later appointments for discussion of the job. Along these same lines, Joan can try to converge to Louise by using language, speech style, and even non-verbal behaviour that are as similar and familiar to Louise as possible. By emphasising the similarities between herself and Louise, she may make the personal relationship more salient, and Louise may be more willing to listen and understand.

Many supervisors believe that understanding is the responsibility of the subordinate, particularly if they come from cultures with strong values of individualism, power equality, and tolerance of uncertainty. They are happy to let the subordinate take the lead and to let go partially of control of how the job is done. They may even believe that checking is insulting to the subordinate, who should be proud to take the initiative for the job. As it turns out, however, even people from individualist cultures are more willing to ask for help when they need it if they have clearly been given permission to do so by those who have power over them, whether the context is work, school, or doctor's office. When subordinates come from cultures that are more collectivist, higher in power distance, or have a lower tolerance for uncertainty, giving permission and explicit encouragement to ask questions may be even more important.

### Making reports and giving feedback on performance

These days, as jobs become more complex and there is more emphasis on multi-skilling, accountability, and efficiency in the workplace, supervisors are asked increasingly often to make judgements about the performance of their subordinates and to communicate this feedback to them. Many supervisors dread this task, especially when some of their subordinates come from other cultures or ethnic groups, and especially when criticism is involved. Giving performance feedback can be a tricky and difficult job, made even more difficult when judgements of appraisal are combined with suggestions for future development and better work practices. Many organisational psychologists and management specialists argue that these two processes should not be combined at all. When the supervisor and subordinate come from different cultures, the likelihood that subordinates will interpret bad news as bias or prejudice—as well as the possibility that a negative judgement is partly due to the supervisor's own cultural biases—is much greater.

It is beyond the scope of this book to give advice on performance feedback as such. What we can say, though, is that the rules and difficulties that operate in all communication between supervisors and subordinates are likely to be exacerbated in intercultural contexts, and the chance of miscommunication is even greater than usual. In addition, in at least some cultures there are rules against giving negative feedback or criticism unless it is expressed indirectly and politely (see Bryan & Gallois, 1992; Wilson & Gallois, 1993). Thus, it is especially important to give clear feedback with specific details and examples of the subordinate's work, as well as many opportunities for checking and questioning. If a plan of action for the future is to be developed, it is essential to get the agreement of both the supervisor and the subordinate about this. If decisions about promotion, probation, or salary are involved, once again the details need to be spelled out clearly.

All these things are essential for good practice within a single culture. They are even more important when two or more cultures are involved. Remember the discussion of face and politeness in Chapter 4; these issues loom large when feedback about performance is given. For example, subordinates from a culture using low-context language may be rather unhappy if the supervisor criticises their work with a bald on-record statement, or if the supervisor makes specific suggestions for improvement, even if the supervisor is careful to include expressions of politeness. Subordinates from cultures that have high-context languages are likely to be completely devastated by this same behaviour, since people go on record (give explicit criticism) in such languages only in very serious situations. There are many unhappy examples of multinational companies that have transferred their performance appraisal systems wholecloth from one country to another without considering the impact of culture, with disastrous results like these.

If the supervisor can find a way to get the point across more indirectly, for example by asking subordinates to make suggestions for themselves about how they could work better, this may help the subordinates to get the message without the overly strong emotional tone. This is not easy to do, however, so supervisors need to be prepared for unexpected reactions and to take extra time and care to make sure they are understood. Once again, converging to the subordinate's language, way of speaking, and style may help to increase receptiveness to what the supervisor is saying.

## Communicating Needs and Desires: Managing Upwards

Let us return to the conversation between Joan and Louise, and think about it this time from Louise's perspective. For her, it seems to be important to make a good impression, to show willingness to work, and in the long run to please her supervisor. Doing the job correctly is a means to this end, but it may not be the most salient or even the most important part of the conversation for her. It is only later, when she gets back to her desk and looks at the case she is supposed to work on, that she realises she has not understood. How does she communicate her need for more information to Joan, when Joan has said she is confident Louise can do it on her own?

Louise's difficulties are the flip side of Joan's—she needs to communicate her need for more information upwards, and to make sure her desires are understood without doing damage to her reputation as a good worker or to her relationship with Joan. Joan, in her turn, has the same problems as Louise when she wishes to communicate her needs and desires to Martin Clementi, her own supervisor. It may be just as difficult for her to ask him questions, and just as hard for Martin to understand why she is reluctant, as it is when Joan is the supervisor and Louise is the subordinate.

It is clear already that there are strong expectations and social rules about how supervisors and subordinates should communicate. It is also clear that these rules differ from one culture to another, as well as from one type of organisation to another, and that the rules can get in the way of clear communication within a culture, and even more so between cultures. What may not be so clear is that it is easier for subordinates than for supervisors to get around these difficulties. This idea jars against our notions about power, which all imply that the more powerful person has more room to move, and thus more chance to get good understanding, in any communication with a less powerful person. We also know from many studies that the more powerful person is more likely to set the communication agenda; that is, to determine what is talked about, how much time is spent on each topic, and so forth (see Ng & Bradac, 1993). How can it be easier for subordinates to enhance understanding?

The reason is simple enough: subordinates need to receive clear information more than supervisors need to give it, because the subordinates are the ones who will ultimately be faced with doing the job. People who need information or who are dependent on someone else for rewards also tend to be more sensitive to the reactions of the more powerful person, which makes it easier for them to initiate communication (see Henley & Kramarae, 1991). In addition, the longer subordinates go before clearing up doubts or misunderstandings, the more face they will lose when they finally have to ask, and the harder it will be to ask. In short, subordinates hold the key to effective communication with supervisors, by managing upwards. Being aware of this may be the biggest thing subordinates can do to help their communication with supervisors, especially when more than one culture is involved.

How Louise should go about asking Joan for more information, or how in another situation Joan should deal with her own supervisor, Martin, depends on the culture and also the rules and expectations of the organisation itself. In the case of this legal firm, there is a high premium on getting the facts right as well as on meeting deadlines imposed by clients, courts, and others. Thus, there is likely to be an expectation that questions should be asked earlier rather than later. Another type of organisation might have a different rule, requiring work by the subordinate first, and questions later to clear up any lingering questions once the bulk of the job is done. In addition, if the firm is in France and Joan is an Anglo-Saxon sojourner (perhaps on a secondment to this branch of the company), Joan is likely to be more willing to tolerate doubt and uncertainty than Louise or Martin. Thus, it is possible that Joan will be more annoyed by questions from Louise than Martin is when Joan asks him for information, and Joan needs to be sensitive to this cultural difference.

In the case of managing upwards, it is important to communicate questions, needs, and desires in ways that preserve the relationship and maintain the face of all involved. As the Anglo-Saxon and French cultures are both relatively individualistic, there should be few problems about asking direct questions and the subordinate's taking the initiative. In more collectivistic cultures, this activity would probably need to take place in private, with careful attention to the face needs of the other person. Given the difference in power, it would be very useful even in individualist cultures to employ politeness strategies and to make it clear that no criticism of the supervisor is meant.

## Intercultural Communication among Colleagues: Managing Across

Finally, we take up the issue of communicating with colleagues, where problems of unequal power are not so obvious. Even here, however, the problems that we have brought up in earlier chapters and sections—the operation of different rules, and the salience of social identity and negative stereotypes—can make it harder to communicate smoothly.

When colleagues from different cultures work together in the same organisational unit, they may interact well because their social identity as members of the unit is more important than their cultural identity. This is likely to happen when their unit is in competition or is having problems with another unit. Solidarity for the work group tends to make the people in it see each other as similar but different from and better than the rival work group, so that differences based on culture, ethnic group, gender, and other large-scale social features are pushed into the background. In such situations, rules and norms specific to the unit develop and tend to take precedence over previously learned cultural rules.

In the course of everyday working life, however, rivalries with other work groups often recede into the background, and social identity based on culture can become more salient, especially at times of stress. Consider the following example:

A large medical practice in Florida employs several people as medical secretaries and receptionists. The practice is an area with a large Latin American population, so two of the secretaries and one of the doctors are Hispanic, and all the secretaries are bilingual in English and Spanish. Each medical practitioner has his or her own secretary, but because the work flow is uneven, they also share work under the informal supervision of the senior partner's secretary, who has the most work experience. When things are really busy, the head secretary (an Anglo) tends to distribute the work by simply telling the others what to do. This annoys all the others, and she has been accused of racism behind her back by the Hispanic secretaries. At the same time, the Anglo secretaries believe the Hispanic secretaries are not pulling their weight, because every time things get really busy, one of them complains that she has too much work, while the other one keeps working without talking at all. The Anglo secretaries feel as though they are working much too hard (one of them complains all the time too, but she is lazy), and they believe the Hispanic secretaries are carrying a far lighter load. In fact, they have complained to the doctors about this on several occasions, which is causing problems for the practice as a whole.

If this practice included people from only one culture, the complaints would probably be explained in two ways. First, there is too much work, because of unpredictable work flow, understaffing, inefficient organisation of the work, or a combination of all these factors, and this is causing stress among the secretaries. Secondly, one of the secretaries is not pulling her weight—she was described above as lazy—and she needs to improve or be replaced. Thirdly, the head secretary may not be communicating effectively in assigning work to the others, or they may not accept her communication as appropriate for her role. Because cultural identity is salient in this example, however, the situation is explained in terms of culture. The Hispanic secretaries think the Anglos are racist, and the Anglos think the Hispanics are somehow getting away with doing less work. Cultural identity is getting in the way of seeing the role played by other factors. Beyond this, different rules about how to distribute work or how to communicate about work flow could also be making the situation more difficult.

In addressing such problems it can be very useful to analyse the situation independently of cultural factors. This is not to say that cultural rules and values are unimportant within a single work unit; obviously they are. On the other hand, many problems in communication within a work unit come about because of organisational factors, and it is essential to understand these factors if the problems are to be addressed effectively. To do this, the impact of cultural identity has to be minimised, so that problems are not immediately explained in terms of it. In addition, when social identity based on culture or ethnic group is very salient, it is much harder to see the differences between individuals. In this example, some secretaries may be carrying the load for others, but they may be unable or unwilling to acknowledge this while the other ethnic group is being held responsible for the problems.

When different work units are also composed of people from different cultures, rivalry and hostility can become intense. Stereotypes about the other unit can become confounded with stereotypes about the other ethnic group. For example, in a university department we know about, the academic staff members are almost all from the United Kingdom, whereas the members of the administrative and technical support staff are all Australians. Interpersonal spoken communication between these two groups has almost ceased, and staff members communicate mainly by means of formal memos and e-mail messages. Meanwhile, among themselves the support staff members refer to the academics in derogatory ethnic terms, as 'toffee-nosed Poms', and in occupational terms as 'typical elitists—what would you expect of a bunch of ivory-tower whingers anyway?' The academics in their turn refer to the support staff as 'like all the so-called support staff—only interested in pushing the paper, not in getting the job done' and as 'little Aussie bludgers', a negative recasting of the common Australian expression of national pride, 'little Aussie battler'. In this kind of case, there are almost certainly different rules operating, but these rules are linked to the organisational role rather than the cultural group. Because cultural identity and organisational role separate these people so neatly into groups, however, one identity builds on another to produce prejudice and miscommunication.

This is the kind of case where good communication is extremely difficult to achieve. The most obvious potential solutions, indeed, do not explicitly involve communication. Working conditions might be improved sufficiently to reduce stress. In addition, the organisational structure might be changed to minimise the differences between academic and support staff; for example, by forming partially independent teaching groups including both academic and support staff. Finally, the composition of the staff may change so that cultural group and staff group are not so closely linked. In the meantime, the staff may be doing the right thing to minimise their face-to-face communication, at least in public. In private, though, it is a different matter. It may be a good strategy for individual members of the two groups to develop personal relationships outside the department. The interpersonal communication between them will at least lower the temperature of some of the intergroup communication, and it stands some chance of being generalised back to the whole group.

## CONCLUSIONS

In summary, communication among people in the workplace involves multiple identities—organisational role and status, identity as a unit member, roles based on experience (new workers versus old hands), gender, as well as cultural identity. All these roles involve social rules, and these rules, like cultural ones, may or may not be in the conscious awareness of the people who follow them or break them. Thus, misunderstanding can be caused by a large number of factors, so that it is no surprise that miscommunication is so common. When intercultural communication is involved, however, often culture is blamed for everything, and the important (sometimes overwhelming) role played by the other factors is forgotten. As we have done in earlier chapters, we finish with a few guidelines which may help you to analyse miscommunication and to repair it in many workplace situations.

1. Be aware that you often cannot predict the social rules that are operating in a work situation, or what identity is behind them.
2. Be aware of your own rules and stereotypes, and the possibility that they are clouding your judgement.
3. Take extra time to make decisions, and gather more information if necessary.
4. Give more opportunities to check, and do more checking, than you think is really necessary.
5. Remember that culture is not the only difference between workers, and it may not be the most important one.
6. Remember that individuals in the same group are different from each other, and resist the temptation to generalise the behaviour of one person to the whole group.

# 7

# INTERCULTURAL COMMUNICATION WITH CLIENTS AND CUSTOMERS

The previous chapter dealt with the impact of culture inside organisational settings. The focus there was especially on colleagues and internal clients, and on meeting their needs. In multicultural workplaces, such interactions consume a great part of the working day. But they do not give the whole picture. At some times, all of us deal with people outside our own organisations—clients, customers, patients, or students. The same sorts of issues that arise in other intercultural encounters occur in these interactions as well. Professionals have a special relationship with their clients, however, because clients and customers are paying for services. This relationship has its own impact on the language and communication used, as well as on the problems that occur. Relationships with clients and customers are the subject of this chapter. As well as examining face-to-face communication between professionals and clients, we will look at mass communication strategies aimed at changing attitudes and behaviour, including health and safety campaigns in multicultural communities.

One might think, as some business people assert, that 'the language of business is the customer's language'. While this is true some of the time and in some circumstances, it is far from universal for managers, lawyers, doctors, or teachers to accommodate to the language and communication styles of their clients. As we examine several types of professional–client relationships, several factors emerge as important in determining who accommodates to whose language and style, and the difficulties and solutions that appear as a result These factors include the following:

1. *The extent of contact over time.* Do the professionals and the client have an ongoing relationship, or is the encounter a one-off?
2. *The importance of the relationship.* How much does the professional need *this particular* client, and how much choice does the client have?
3. *Power.* Is the professional or the client in the more powerful position in this encounter and this relationship? Do both people agree about who is more powerful?
4. *The type of task.* What is it, and how important is it to get the task done efficiently and well?
5. *The skills of the people involved.* How much does the professional know about the client's language, communication style, values? How much does the client know about the professional's?
6. *The message that needs to be delivered.* What are the consequences of the information being given for the client? Is there bad news, or something that must be discussed in a very personal way?

As we explore relationships between professionals and their customers, medical patients, students, and other clients, keep these factors in mind.

## BUSINESS TRANSACTIONS: IS THE CUSTOMER ALWAYS RIGHT?

Business transactions that involve the selling of products or services are a clear case where the customer or buyer has power over the seller, and thus where the seller is likely to accommodate to the customer's language and communication style, as well as to the cultural rules and values that underlie them. There are many cases where this is so. For example, European business people frequently state the belief that they should do business in the customer's language. This practice is widely used in Europe, and it has developed many of the features of diglossia among multilingual managers. In this case, the language of choice changes depending upon who is selling and who is buying; it is the buyer's language. In addition, retail establishments like hotels and shops in tourist areas all over the world make sure that they have staff who can speak the main languages of tourists, and businesses that can provide this service tend to sell more (see Sparks, 1995). Some businesses, particularly in the retail and tourist sectors, may import people from the major customer groups to act as guides and salespeople in the host country. Practices like these say something about what it is to be a tourist. The motivation to visit the new country may be more to have a good time than to learn about the environment or interact with the natives (Pearce, 1982).

Even in apparently straightforward situations like these, however, considerations of power and social identity can intrude. For example, in French-speaking Quebec, shop assistants in the early 1980s were prepared to accommodate to English-speaking customers (Genesee & Bourhis, 1982). Later in the decade, people in Quebec had begun to favour a different rule: answer in French first to an English-speaking customer, then accommodate later if necessary (Genesee & Bourhis, 1988). By then, the intergroup relations between Francophones and Anglophones in Canada were hotter, and the social identity of French speakers in Quebec prescribed sticking with the home language.

This Canadian example shows the ways in which language can be used to signal social identity in transactions with customers, especially where there is a history of conflict or inequality between two cultural groups. Sometimes, this goes as far as a seller adamantly refusing to speak the language of a buyer. A friend of ours was visiting Belgium some years ago and went into a restaurant in the city of Leuven/Louvain. The proprietor let him know that she couldn't speak French and that anyway the restaurant was closed. When he responded in English that he couldn't speak French himself, she welcomed him in and served him an excellent meal. As is often the case, the issue here was not the language as such, but what the language signified about the group memberships of the speakers. Another process with similar motivation can occur in tourist areas, where sellers may accommodate to the language of their foreign customers, but show their resentment of this situation by charging higher prices or disadvantaging their customers in other ways.

In larger-scale business negotiations, language accommodation represents a significant signal of power. The person who accommodates acknowledges the power of the other person, the prestige of the other person's language, and his or her own desire to be approved of by the other group (see Gallois & Callan, 1991; Giles & Coupland, 1991). Thus, political negotiators often use interpreters even when they are fluent in each other's languages. This practice, as well as ensuring exact translations in sometimes sensitive situations, also exerts the power and prestige of the home language. Of course, such acknowledgements can become an important chip in the bargaining process, as switching to the other person's language can put him or her under some obligation. For these reasons, it is in the interests of people trading in other cultures to make sure that they, or at least some people on the negotiating team, have command of the other language and can use it if necessary. Interestingly, there are frequent cases where companies in business negotiations can actually understand the language of the other party but do not disclose this information, in the hope of having an advantage at the bargaining table.

## OTHER KINDS OF CLIENTS

When we move away from customers who are buying goods or services to other types of clients, even those who pay for what they receive, the situation changes dramatically. First, the professionals who provide these services are aware of their own social power and prestige, and they use it (often unconsciously) in their interactions with clients. Furthermore, in most of these cases the language of the host culture, and the values and communication style that go with it, are dominant: the rule seems to be, 'When in Rome, do as the Romans do'. Unfortunately, clients are not always able to do this, and some of the major problems of intercultural communication arise in interactions between native-born professionals and immigrant or sojourner clients. Let us give a few examples.

CASE 1. A doctor is seeing a female patient who does not speak the language of the host country, and the doctor does not speak the patient's language. The patient has brought along her teen-aged daughter to translate. The problem is serious and delicate, and the daughter appears to be very embarrassed by the whole situation. The doctor is pretty sure that the daughter is not translating all of the doctor's questions, or giving back all of the detail in the mother's answers, but she doesn't know how to break through the block to get the information needed. The doctor can make her best guess and prescribe a treatment on the information available, but the mother's health depends on getting the diagnosis right.

CASE 2. A client comes to see a solicitor with a complaint about the behaviour of a neighbour. The client is an immigrant with some knowledge of the host language, but the solicitor suspects that part of the problem is that the client and the neighbour have had a major misunderstanding of some kind. He believes that the complaint would be best handled through mediation, rather than starting a complicated and costly legal process which may not succeed, and which will cause him, as well as the client, many problems. He has no idea how he can convince the client of this.

CASE 3. A very angry parent comes to see a school teacher with the complaint that his son has been degraded by being bossed around by a female teacher's aide. The father, an immigrant, is very fluent in the host country's language, but he appears to subscribe to a very different cultural rule about behaviour between women and men. The teacher tries to explain that, in her country, this is the way things are done and the boy will have to comply, but the father remains angry and says he will take the complaint further. The teacher wants to defuse the situation before things go too far, because a complaint like this will reflect badly on her and the school, as well as potentially harming the student. She doesn't know how to negotiate this situation.

CASE 4. A small group of foreign students are together in the same undergraduate course. They often ask questions after class, but rarely speak during the class sessions. The native-born students in the class complain to the lecturer that these students are taking up an unfair amount of the lecturer's time and attention. At the same time, the foreign students complain to the head of department that the lecturer is discriminating against them and that the whole class is racist. The lecturer and the head of department are at a loss as to how to reconcile this conflict.

Problems like these are very common in situations where immigrants, sojourners, or sometimes even short-term visitors are involved. From the discussions in earlier chapters, we can point immediately to several similar features in these four examples. First, they all probably involve different rules or cultural values. Secondly, they all concern questions or disputes about who has the most power, and who should accommodate. Should the lecturer in Case 4 give the foreign students even more attention (accommodate to their communication needs), or should she accommodate to the demands of the native-born students, who may indeed be prejudiced against the foreigners? In Case 3, should the school treat the immigrant boy and others like him differently in order to acknowledge the values of his home culture, and in the process of accommodating risk compromising some of the values and rules of their own culture? Thirdly, all four cases involve important issues about social identity. Each of them portrays people who feel some need to defend their own cultural identity against perceived threats from outside. Note that it is enough for the threats to be *perceived by one person* for a problem to arise; the other person may not have any awareness of a threat or problem. Let us examine each of the above cases in turn.

## Doctors and Patients

In the first case, the daughter is caught in the middle of a situation for which she does not have adequate training or experience. She wants to help her mother, but she does not know how to handle the delicate conversation, and so reacts to her own discomfort instead of staying with the task at hand. On top of this, she may also be caught between the old culture (her mother's) and the new one in which she has spent much of her life, so that she is embarrassed by her mother's lack of language skills and reacts by giving her minimal or grudging help (see Callan, Gallois & Forbes, 1983). At the same time, the doctor may wish to help and to treat the patient properly, but may also believe that it is the task of immigrants to learn the host language and rules (see Kim, 1988). The doctor may unintentionally show her frustration and resentment to the daughter, thus causing her even more discomfort.

In this situation, the doctor is the most powerful person. In the first place, she has the social power and prestige accorded to people with expertise in medicine. In addition, the patient is likely to need her help more than she needs that particular patient. The doctor also has more knowledge of the cultural rules and the medical system than the mother or the daughter. She needs to make use of her power to help the daughter out of her difficult situation. She might, for example, suggest bringing in an outside interpreter or telephone interpreter. She could even invoke a professional rule that interpreters rather than family members should be used for case consultations, as this is indeed a rule for medical practice in many multicultural countries. The daughter is likely to support this course of action even if the mother does not, and the two of them together may well convince the mother. In insisting on a professional interpreter, the doctor is insisting that the patient's family accommodates to her own rules for practice, rather than accommodating to their desire to keep the problem in the family. By doing this, however, she will probably be in a better position to meet the patient's needs in the long run.

## Lawyers and Clients

Case 2 is very similar to Case 1, in that the solicitor's task is to get the client to see the solution his way, because he believes that this is in the best interests of the client. In other words, like the doctor, he must get the client to accommodate to his rules for practice, not so much to advance his own identity and power but to help the client. This is a complicated type of accommodation, and the risk is that the solicitor will be seen as patronising and as ordering the client around. Again, however, the social situation and his knowledge of both the culture and the legal system give him more power than perhaps he realises in the situation. He is also likely to have power because the client needs his services more than he needs this particular client; indeed, his belief that he should send the client to mediation testifies to this. Nevertheless, he needs to be patient and to try to see the situation from the client's point of view: the client has probably come in looking for a quick and successful solution to the problem, and this is not going to happen. In fact, knowing that he has more power in this situation may well give him the confidence to treat the client in a considerate and non-defensive way.

## Teachers, Students, and the Community

Cases 3 and 4 are slightly different, in that they involve more people, and also because the social power dynamics are not quite so straightforward. In Case 3, the father needs the school for his child, but the school also needs the goodwill of the parents, so each side has power over the other. The teacher has more knowledge of the host culture and the educational system, but the father does appear to understand his rights as a citizen of a democratic country and as a parent. In addition, the teacher may be constrained because the student is not the only person affected by what she does—if she treats him differently from the others, the result may be complaints from other parents.

Even though there is more complexity in this case, the situation will still probably be most easily resolved if the teacher can convince the father to accommodate to the rules of the host country. To do this, she will probably have to listen carefully, without defending herself, to his point of view, and to acknowledge his right to feel the way he does. Once she has heard him out, it should be easier for her to explain the rules in her country and the reasons for them, and to do so in a way that will not threaten the face of the father. By listening to him, in fact, she may discover that face is the major issue for him—first, because his son was treated in what for him was a rule-violating manner, and then because he wants his side to be heard and respected. Once that happens, he may be prepared to accept the cultural difference and the need to accommodate to it. If he does not agree, or if other parents from his cultural group support his stance, this is a sign that deeper social identity issues may be involved. At this point, the educational authority may need to make a policy decision about whether to accommodate or not. Here, the decision may rest on how important the cultural value is. Most of the time, however, the problem can be resolved at a lower level, without invoking formal policy.

Case 4 is complicated too, but for a different reason. This case illustrates how much racism and discrimination rest in the eye of the beholder. The foreign students are probably working very hard and are keen to succeed at their new university. Typically, their visas and financial assistance depend on success. They are also likely to be working hard to understand the rules and values of the host culture, and in fact to be more sensitive and sophisticated about the differences between their home culture and the new one than the native-born students are (Kim; 1988; Scott & Scott, 1989). They may be doing their best to accommodate to these new rules. This could even be the source of their trouble. For example, they may have noticed that the native-born students freely ask questions in class, but they may be hesitant to do this themselves because of their own social rules or because of their worries about their competence in the new language (Barker et al., 1991). Therefore, they imitate the behaviour of the native students (ask lots of questions), but they do it after class in a less public way. Because they are so eager to succeed, they may not be aware that they are over-accommodating— going too far in asking the lecturer's advice. On the other hand, the native-born students are all too aware of this.

The lecturer and head of department need to take account of one important feature of social identity: it is made much more salient by stress. The stress for the foreign students comes from their desire to succeed and the strangeness of a new country (Gudykunst, 1991). All the students may feel stress because of their workload, the difficulty of the course, or the competitiveness in their university programme. The more threatened they feel, the more likely they are to lash out at another ethnic or cultural group (or indeed, at any group that is different from them in some noticeable way). Thus, there

may be a solution to the problem that circumvents the immediate issues but reduces the stress. It may be possible to lower
the students' anxiety by explaining the assessment more fully,
reducing the workload (for example, by giving the students
more time to complete their work), or building the students'
confidence that they will succeed in the course. These possibilities, of course, depend on the context of the course and
the university.

Beyond reducing stress, the lecturer may be able to change the
social identity situation in another way: by creating or emphasising a new identity that includes both the native-born and the
foreign students (see Vaughan & Hogg, 1995). The same action
can also be applied to Case 3. For example, the lecturer can
introduce activities or discussion that emphasise the social
identity of students, or that imply competition with students in
other classes or other courses, rather than within the one class.
This could also involve cooperative work or group-based assessment. In doing this, it may be important for the students to
retain their original identity, so that they now work from two
identities in this context: their common identity as students in
this class, and their cultural identity. The lecturer may even be
able to point to the extra resources the class has because of its
multicultural membership. This way, the students develop an
important new identity that allows them to cooperate without
the fear of losing the old one. In these circumstances of cooper-
ation, we have found in our own research with Chinese and
Australian students and lecturers that ethnic group membership is far less important in determining communicative behaviour and judgements about it than are status and the task at
hand (Jones et al., 1994, 1995).

## Foreign Teaching Assistants

In all these examples, the client, or the person buying the
service from the professional, is an immigrant or sojourner.
What about the situation where the shoe is on the other foot—

where the professional is from another culture, and the client is from the host country? Here the social rules and power dynamics have different features. We will illustrate this situation with the case of foreign teaching assistants (instructors or tutors) in universities, but it applies equally well to the case of foreign doctors, engineers, or other professional people.

Many universities, especially in Western countries with a large number of foreign postgraduate students, employ these students as tutors or teaching assistants in their undergraduate classes. Often, the reaction of the undergraduates is to say, 'Oh no!' and to drop the class at the first opportunity (Rao, 1995; Bresnahan & Cai, 1995). The complaint is that they cannot understand the teaching assistants and their work will suffer as a result. Usually, the undergraduate students complain that the teaching assistant's knowledge of the language is not good enough to teach the course properly. Is this really what is going on?

Some research on impressions of foreign instructors has found that their accented speech is perceived as less competent and harder to understand than exactly the same words spoken by a person with a native accent (Rao, 1995; Rubin, 1995). These findings are very similar to other work on language attitudes (see Gallois & Callan, 1986; Giles & Coupland, 1991; Ryan & Giles, 1982). What seems to happen is that the teaching assistant's foreign accent makes the students' cultural identity salient, and they 'tune out' to what the other person is saying. This is a problem in many contexts, as we have seen in earlier chapters, but it is a special problem here because of the stress students feel. As we noted earlier, they are eager to succeed, and very conscious of the pressure to do well. In addition, the instructor has power over them, because this person is a major source of information about the course and because the instructor may be involved in assessing their work. So they blame the teaching assistant for their stress, and explain their problems in terms of the instructor's inadequacy instead of acknowledging their own fears and concerns. They are so concerned about the teaching assistant's language that they cannot get the benefit of the person's knowledge and skill. In their turn, the foreign teaching assistants may blame their own difficulties with their teaching or their other work as postgraduate students on the prejudice and hostility of the native-born students.

We are back to Case 4 above. Because of the roles of students and teacher, however, the solution must be different. In this kind of case, the teaching assistant is under a strong obligation to accommodate. These teachers need to be well trained in the host culture's rules about behaviour in academic contexts, in the host language, and in intercultural communication skills, as well as in their own area of expertise. Many universities do train their foreign teaching assistants in these skills, and their efforts pay off in better relations between teaching assistants and their students. In this case, it is important for the teaching assistants to accommodate *in spite of* the power they have over students, and because they need the students as much as the students need them. Similarly, other professionals who are dependent on clients from another culture may need to make the extra effort to accommodate, particularly when they are foreigners.

On the other hand, there is also benefit in training clients to appreciate the efforts of professionals from other cultures, in those cases where it is possible to do so. Universities and schools are examples of contexts where such training is possible, and a number of universities have developed brief programmes in intercultural communication training for their undergraduates (Mark, 1995). These programmes tackle the issue of prejudice head-on, as well as using the sorts of techniques we describe in this book to sensitise students to differences in cultural rules. Their goal is to persuade the students to give the foreign teaching assistants a chance to show what they can do. Once this happens, the teaching assistants are in a better position to succeed on their own merits. To achieve this goal, the twin issues of social rules and social identity must be dealt with together—dealing with one alone will probably not be enough.

# MASS COMMUNICATION AND CULTURE

Up to this point, we have considered interactions between professionals and clients that take place face-to-face, or perhaps over the telephone. Some of the same points about accommodation in language are also relevant to written communication like letters, faxes, and e-mail (see Chapter 4). There are many occasions, however, when this kind of interpersonal communication does not occur, but where clients are reached through mass communications media, including newsletters, poster campaigns, and television. A major example of this kind of communication is disease prevention and health campaigns, which target whole communities and attempt to persuade people to be vaccinated, practice safe sex, eat healthier diets, stay out of the sun, and so forth. It is easy to forget the role of culture in contexts like these, but culture plays a vital role in the success of the campaigns.

## Culture, Values, and HIV Prevention

The discovery of AIDS in 1981 and the subsequent pandemic have made the prevention of HIV transmission a key health issue in every country in the world. Mass communication campaigns on safe sex and other HIV-preventive practices have taken place on every continent. Because HIV is mainly a sexually transmitted disease, educators realised early on that cultural values about sexual practice and sex roles would be an important factor in the success of the campaigns. Nevertheless, early in the epidemic the campaigns were driven by Western research and reflected Western cultural values. In the past six or seven years, the crucial importance of locally relevant communication has become much more obvious. Let us give a few examples.

In most Western cultures, sexual decisions are thought of as the domain of individual people; they are each person's responsibility. Thus, the HIV-prevention campaigns that appeared on television, radio, and in print emphasised individual responsibility. The message was that 'you owe it to yourself to protect yourself from HIV infection' and that 'only you can practice safe sex'. This message is congruent with Western values, in particular the high value put on individualism. It is also compatible with the belief that sex is private and under the control of individual people, and with the belief that safe behaviour will reduce risk. In the West, the challenge has been to convince people that they are at personal risk of infection and that they need to do something about their risk. This is particularly true because, in the West, AIDS has been associated with minority groups like drug users and homosexual men.

The story is quite different in Africa, still the major site of the epidemic. Here, sexual decision-making is not so private, and is discussed more freely than in most Western countries. On the other hand, many African cultures are more collectivist, and place more emphasis on the importance of family life. For these reasons, the Western-driven mass communications fell rather flat in Africa. They were too prudish about sex, and they relied too much on convincing individuals to 'do the right thing'. In more recent years, HIV-prevention campaigns in Africa, and in other communities with similar attitudes and values about sex and the family, have relied more on emphasising a person's obligation to the family ('If you get sick, what will your family do?') and less on self-protection. In addition, these campaigns have taken a frank and rather humorous approach to sex, something that would probably not be culturally acceptable in many Western countries.

This example brings us back to high-context and low-context language, a key feature in mass communication. As we noted in earlier chapters, cultures tend more to high-context or low-context communication (Gudykunst & Ting-Toomey, 1988; Hall,

1976). What needs to be spelled out explicitly in English or German can be implied in Thai or Chinese. We also noted, however, that all languages have some high-context areas and some low-context ones. As the HIV-prevention campaigns show, sexual practice is a paradoxical area, in that Western languages are unusually high context here, whereas languages that are normally high context may be quite explicit in this area.

How can we get the language right in an area like HIV prevention, which involves the core values of most cultures and is frightening into the bargain? Probably the only way to do this well is to do it in collaboration with the local group that is being targeted by the campaign. For example, in Australia HIV-prevention campaigns aimed at Australian Aborigines have been conducted mainly by Aboriginal health workers, who themselves have worked hard in local communities to get the language right, to make use of knowledge and concepts that are relevant to the communities, to use humour, and to tap into cultural identities and values that are compatible with the message. In the USA, very different kinds of campaigns have been developed for highly individualistic Anglos and very family-oriented Hispanics, once again with the participation of people in the relevant communities. It is important for those developing the campaigns to keep in mind that no one approach will work for everyone, even within a single community if the community is multicultural.

## Mass Communication and Cultural Identity

What is true for HIV-prevention campaigns is equally true in other areas, whether it is health maintenance, education about rights or rules, or mass communication for entertainment. The style must be right, and the organisation of the message must be appropriate to the people who will receive it. When Westerners read newspaper articles written by Koreans, for example, they often find it difficult to 'get the message', because the articles do not have the logical ordering that they expect.

The same thing happens in reverse. A logical, explicit message that begins with a topic sentence, works towards a clear conclusion, and ends with a take-home message can be completely lost on a person who is used to writing around the point until eventually the reader understands it—a typical high-context strategy.

Even closely related languages like English and French are different in this way, with English paragraph construction often going in almost the reverse order to the preferred construction in French. In addition, the meaning of words changes subtly from one language to another (Lambert, Havelka & Crosby, 1959). This may be one reason why the bilingual author Julien Green felt that he had to rewrite his books from scratch, rather than translate them from French into English (Ervin-Tripp, 1964). Virtually the only way to achieve the right style is to work with people from the local culture. Direct translation may get you by in face-to-face interactions, but more than this is necessary for mass communication, where there is little or no chance for the person who receives the message to check it out. The receivers will interpret the message they receive. It is important that they interpret it in something like the way it was intended by the sender.

## CONCLUSIONS

This chapter has pointed to some of the complexities that come into communication with people outside of organisations. Clients and customers cannot be expected to have the cultural competence that professionals may be under an obligation to attain. Thus, there are a number of important guidelines for practice, that are somewhat different from contexts where power and knowledge are more equal:

1. Be aware that the service deliverer usually has greater social power in interactions with clients—use this power to help the client.

2. Reach out to the clients, and accommodate as much as possible to their knowledge and motivation to understand the message.
3. Tailor messages to the values and attitudes of clients, rather than your own values.
4. Use the language and communication style of clients wherever possible.
5. Where interpreters are needed, make sure they are fully trained.

Even with the differences, many of the same skills that are applied in interactions between professionals, or between people in the same organisation, can be applied in these contexts too. In the last chapter, we will present a final set of guidelines for practice in intercultural contexts.

# 8

# USING INTERCULTURAL COMMUNICATION SKILLS: CONCLUSIONS AND STRATEGIES

In this final chapter, we will sum up the major issues we have dealt with throughout the book, and present some overall strategies which professionals can use to help minimise difficulties in encounters with people from other cultures. We have pointed to several common problems in earlier chapters, including

— misunderstandings between people from different cultures
— uncertainty about what the rules are in a new culture
— uncertainty about what the other person is thinking or feeling
— clashes of values
— bias, prejudice, or hostility between people from different cultures.

In considering these issues one more time, we will take up three questions:

1. How can we prevent miscommunication in intercultural encounters?

2. When misunderstanding or miscommunication does occur, how can we minimise its negative impact on us and on others?
3. How can we reduce the impact of prejudice, bias, and hostility between people based on cultural group membership?

## Preventing Miscommunication

As we have pointed out many times in this book, misunderstandings and communication repair are the stuff of everyday conversations even within a single culture, especially when we talk to people outside our immediate families and close friends. Most of the time, such misunderstandings cause only minor problems, and sometimes they are repaired so quickly we do not even notice them. Even so, misunderstandings are more likely across cultures, because it is more likely that the rules are different. People in different cultures use different communication codes, which involve far more than language. This potential source of difficulty can in fact be an asset, if we use our knowledge about social rules to keep from jumping too quickly to conclusions about what others mean and think. Thus, in any intercultural encounter, it is important to remember that

— the other person does not share all our values and social rules;
— beyond the most general level, it is likely to be impossible to tell in advance where differences in rules and values lie—there are no cross-cultural rule books (including this book);
— people tend to believe that their own rules and values are right and natural;
— most of the time, people do not talk about their rules and values, and sometimes they refuse to talk about them even when asked.

Given all these factors, it is not surprising that surprises, and sometimes shocks, are the norm rather than the exception in intercultural encounters, even when the cultures are closely related, but especially when they are not. To keep these surprises from developing into serious misunderstandings, it is important to try to take the perspective of the other person: to try to see the situation from the other's point of view as well as from our own. To start this process, it is important always *to be on the alert for differences in rules*, so that when they occur the surprise is less. There are several good strategies for doing this:

1. Use your knowledge that cultures are different along major value dimensions and that these value differences have direct consequences for language, non-verbal behaviour, and other social rules.
2. Listen and observe actively, taking in both words and non-verbal behaviour.
3. Form hypotheses (or at least educated guesses) about the specific rules and values in the other person's culture.
4. Where possible, check your hypotheses by asking the other person about rules and values, or by using other sources of information (people, books, mass media).
5. Remember that your hypotheses are just that—they are guesses and inferences about what the other person may be thinking; they are not facts.

When something happens that surprises you, or when your own behaviour does not get the reaction you intended, it is important to consider several alternative explanations for what has happened. In particular, you need to keep in mind that the other person may be responding in terms of another set of rules. This is not the only possibility, however. Intercultural encounters involve more uncertainty and ambiguity than similar interactions within a culture—things are not as clear as we would like, and we tend to be very conscious of this fact. In addition, intercultural travel and communication can be stressful in itself, and we need to pay a great deal of attention to managing the basics. Thus, it is easier to miss an important part of the other person's communication, or to misinterpret something in the situation, simply because we are working harder to keep the encounter going. And there are many other possibilities. To deal with this complexity, we need a set of strategies to prevent misunderstandings:

1. Slow the process down—take the time to think about alternative reasons for the other person's behaviour—use your general knowledge about cultural differences.
2. Always be aware of the rules in your own culture and the untested assumptions you are making about the other person—use your specific knowledge of your own culture.
3. Give the other person the benefit of the doubt—you may be very pleasantly surprised when you discover what he or she really meant.
4. Observe carefully—try to increase your stock of specific knowledge about this culture.
5. If necessary, check with the other person to see if you have understood correctly *before* you act on your assumptions and hypotheses.
6. Be proactive—use the social power you have in the situation to act in the other person's and your own best interests.

## Minimising the Negative Impact of Miscommunication

With the best will in the world, the strategies described above will work some of the time, but not all of the time. Thus, it is important not to be disappointed if they fail and a serious misunderstanding does occur—one that upsets you, someone from your own culture (or organisation), or someone from another culture. Simply being prepared for misunderstandings can take some of the sting out of them when they arise. At the same time, it is useful to have a set of strategies for dealing with these more complex and difficult situations. These strategies should include the following:

1. Give other people the benefit of the doubt—assume that they did not intend to upset you any more than you intended to upset them.
2. Assume that you are more aware of the problem than the other person—you probably are, and even if you are not, you can still act in the other person's interests. Use your general knowledge about cultural values and rules.
3. Slow down enough to consider as many alternative explanations for the other person's behaviour as you can, but do not assume that you have thought of all the possibilities—there may be a reason for the other person's behaviour that will never occur to you.
4. Go lower context—explain the reasons for your own behaviour, without defending yourself as being correct. Use your specific knowledge of your own culture.
5. Check with the other person about whether you have understood his or her behaviour correctly.
6. Where you can, converge to the other person's behaviour; that is, try to follow the other person's communication rules if you can. Use your specific knowledge of the other culture.
7. Be more polite than you normally would—keep in mind that misunderstandings hurt mainly because they threaten someone's face.
8. Be aware of your own cultural bottom line—those values and rules that you simply cannot compromise.

The first and last strategies are the most important. Giving others the benefit of the doubt means that you will not assume they are malicious, prejudiced against you, or trying to win against you when in fact they are not doing any of these things. In the minority of cases where the other person really does have bad motives, you will find out soon enough, and you will have the satisfaction of knowing you did the best you could. Being very polite is part of this same process. In this way, you can minimise threats to face, and you will also encourage the other person to reciprocate by being polite to you.

It may appear that the last strategy, being aware of your own cultural bottom line, contradicts the other strategies. How can we converge, be polite, and give the other person the benefit of the doubt, while at the same time stand up for our own most important values and rules? In fact, the contradiction is more apparent than real. By being aware of our own bottom line, we become conscious of the places where we cannot compromise—the values and rules that are so important that we would prefer to lose the client or leave the culture rather than change them. It is important to do this in order to function effectively in another culture without feeling that our values are being trampled upon. At the same time, however, we become more aware of the many places where compromise or change is possible. As we noted earlier, most cultural rules are arbitrary at least to some extent. We follow them because we have learned to do so, and we do not think much about how important they really are. Once we examine them, it can be very easy to change in order to meet the special demands of intercultural encounters. This is an important part of developing an intercultural perspective and communication style (see Brislin & Yoshida, 1994; Kim, 1995).

## Minimising the Negative Consequences of Prejudice and Bias

But what about the hard cases—the misunderstandings that all the politeness in the world will not fix? What about the times when someone from another culture seems to *want* to misunderstand, or seems to be prejudiced against us? What about the times when we ourselves want to misunderstand, because of our own prejudice or vested interests? As we have pointed out, such situations do occur, and even though they are fortunately in the minority, it is important to acknowledge them and to deal with them when they do arise.

The first step in dealing with prejudice is to be aware that it is ubiquitous (Tajfel, 1979). Our social identities and group memberships are very important to us. It is also important to our self-esteem to see our groups as superior, especially when the situation is threatening or competitive. In cases where the social structure gives our group more power than another group—for example, when our culture is the dominant one in a country and the other person is an immigrant or a member of a less dominant culture—it may be important to us to pre-serve this advantage. On the other hand, when we have less power, we may be very motivated to improve our situation. For example, members of a multinational organisation in a foreign culture may try hard to invoke their own cultural or organisational rules in order to reduce the advantage they perceive local organisations to have. We cannot wish such prejudice away, but we can minimise its negative impact. Once again, we can summarise the points in earlier chapters in terms of a number of strategies, all of which have the goal of *making the communication less intergroup and more interpersonal*:

1. Examine the context. Work to reduce the aspects of the situation—time, pressure, work loads, organisational structure—that are increasing stress level.
2. Think about how hard and closed the boundaries between the groups are, and where they can be crossed more easily.
3. Be aware of the role played by other group memberships besides culture—gender, organisational position, and the like. Do these groups overlap with culture, or is there an-other way to categorise the people in the situation?
4. Be aware that social identity affects some individuals more than others: some people tend to communicate in a more interpersonal way, whereas others are more intergroup.
5. Change your own stereotypes of the other culture by try-ing not to generalise the bad behaviour of one person to the whole group—but do generalise good behaviour to the whole culture.
6. As much as possible, communicate in terms of a larger identity—organisational, role-based, and so forth—which you and the other person share.

7. Use the strategies described above to treat the other person as an individual rather than as a representative of the other culture.
8. As much as possible, converge to the other person's behaviour, in order to encourage him or her to reciprocate and to treat you as an individual.

All of these strategies will help, and they may get you through a situation where prejudice would otherwise have poisoned the interaction. They may also help to reduce prejudice between cultures where it exists, but this is usually a long and slow process. The best you can achieve in these difficult cases is to have a good interpersonal interaction with some of the people in the other culture. But this is a success—you will be more effective than you would have been otherwise, and in the long run you may well help to improve the situation for other people too.

## CONCLUSION

We hope the guidelines in this book will help you to achieve more successful intercultural communication. Experience will also help you—when it comes to communication across cultures, there is no better teacher. The insights brought by research in cross-cultural psychology and communication can equip you better, by giving you a larger perspective on cultural differences and similarities, and by reminding you that everyone has good, culturally based, reasons for behaviour. Nevertheless, it is practice and repeated contact that will refine your communication skills and give you the specific knowledge about another culture and the people in it which you need to be a sophisticated communicator in that culture. What we can say is that you will be successful much of the time, and that when things do not go well, you can feel happy that you did the best you could. Expect to make mistakes, but be confident that you can repair them. Enjoy your intercultural travels!

# REFERENCES

Adams, D. (1980). *The Hitchhiker's Guide to the Galaxy.* New York: Harmony Books.

Argyle, M. (1988). *Bodily Communication* (2nd edn). London: Methuen.

Argyle, M. & Henderson, M. (1985). *The Anatomy of Relationships and the Rules and Skills needed to Manage them Successfully.* London: Methuen.

Argyle, M., Furnham, A. & Graham, I.A. (1981). *Social Situations.* Cambridge: Cambridge University Press.

Argyle, M., Henderson, M., Bond, N., Iizuka, Y. & Contarello, A. (1986). Cross-cultural variations in relationship rules. *International Journal of Psychology,* **21**, 287–315.

Argyle, M., Shimoda, K. & Ricci-Bitti, P. (1978). The intercultural recognition of emotional expressions by three national racial groups: English, Italian and Japanese. *European Journal of Social Psychology,* **8**(2), 169–179.

Ball, P., Giles, H., Byrne, J.L. & Berechree, P. (1984). Situational constraints on the evaluative significance of speech accommodation: Some Australian data. *International Journal of the Sociology of Language,* **46**, 115–129.

Barker, M., Child, C., Gallois, C., Jones, E. & Callan, V.J. (1991). Difficulties of overseas students in social and academic situations. *Australian Journal of Psychology,* **46**, 79–84.

Berger C.R. & Bradac, J.J. (1982). *Language and Social Knowledge.* London: Edward Arnold.

Bochner, S. (Ed.) (1982). *Cultures in Contact: Studies in Cross-cultural Interaction.* New York: Pergamon.

Bochner, S. (1986). Coping with unfamiliar cultures: Adjustments or culture learning? Special issue: contributions to cross-cultural psychology. *Australian Journal of Psychology,* **38**, 347–358.

Bochner, S. (1994). Cross-cultural differences in the self concept: A test of Hofstede's individualism/collectivism distinction. *Journal of Cross-Cultural Psychology,* **25**, 273–283.

Bond, M.H. & Forgas, J.P. (1984). Linking person perception to behavior intention across cultures: The role of cultural collectivism. *Journal of Cross-Cultural Psychology*, **15**, 337–352.

Bourhis, R.Y., Giles, H., Leyens, J.P. & Tajfel, H. (1979). Psycholinguistic distinctiveness: Language divergence in Belgium. In H. Giles & R. St Clair (Eds), *Language and Social Psychology* (pp. 158–185). Oxford: Blackwell.

Bresnahan, M. & Cai, D.A. (1995). The role of aggression in lack of receptivity toward international teaching assistants. Paper presented at the Annual Conference of the International Communication Association, Albuquerque, NM, 25–29 May.

Brigham, J.C. (1977). The structure of racial attitudes of Blacks. *Personality and Social Psychology Bulletin*, **3**, 658–661.

Brislin, R. & Yoshida, T. (1994). *Intercultural Communication Training: An Introduction*. Thousand Oaks, CA: Sage.

Brown, P. & Levinson, S.C. (1978, 1987). *Politeness: Some Universals in Language Usage* (1st and 2nd edns). Cambridge: Cambridge University Press.

Brown, R. & Gilman, A. (1960). The pronouns of power and solidarity. In T. A. Sebeok (Ed.), *Style in Language*. New York: Wiley.

Bryan, A. & Gallois, C. (1992). Rules about assertion in the workplace: Effects of status and message type. *Australian Journal of Psychology*, **44**, 51–60.

Buck, R. (1988). *Human Motivation and Emotion* (2nd edn). New York: Wiley.

Bugental, D.B. (1993). Communication in abusive relationships: Constructions of interpersonal power. *American Behavioral Scientist* (Special Issue on Using and Abusing Language, edited by J. Wiemann & H. Giles), **36**, 288–308.

Burgoon, J.K., Buller, D.B. & Woodall, W.G. (1995). *Nonverbal Communication: The Unspoken Dialogue* (2nd edn). New York: McGraw-Hill.

Burgoon, J.K., Stern, L.A. & Dillman, L. (1995). *Interpersonal Adaptation: Dyadic Interaction Patterns*. New York: Cambridge University Press.

Callan, V.J. & Gallois, C. (1982). Language attitudes of Italo-Australian and Greek Australian bilinguals. *International Journal of Psychology*, **17**, 345–358.

Callan, V.J. & Gallois, C. (1983). Ethnic stereotypes: Australian and Southern European youth. *Journal of Social Psychology*, **119**, 287–288.

Callan, V.J., Gallois, C. & Forbes, P. (1983). Evaluative reactions to accented English: Ethnicity, sex role, and context. *Journal of Cross-Cultural Psychology*, **14**, 407–426.

Cappella, J.N. (1993). The facial feedback hypothesis in human inter-action. *Journal of Language and Social Psychology*, **12**, 13–29.

Cargile, A.C., Giles, H. & Clément, R. (in press). The role of language in ethnic conflict. In J. Gittler (Ed.), *Conflict Knowledge and Conflict Resolution*. Greenwich, CT: JAI Press.

Crawford, M. (1988). Gender, age, and the social evaluation of assertion. *Behavior Modification*, **12**, 549–564.

Eades, D. (1982). You gotta know how to talk . . .: Information seeking in South East Queensland Aboriginal society. *Australian Journal of Linguistics*, **2**, 61–82.

Efron, D. (1941). *Gesture and Environment*. New York: King's Crown Press.

Ekman, P. (1972). Universals and cultural differences in facial expressions of emotion. In J. Cole (Ed.), *Nebraska Symposium on Motivation, 1971* (Vol. 19, pp. 207–283). Lincoln, NE: University of Nebraska Press.

Ekman, P. (Ed.) (1982). *Emotion in the Human Face* (2nd edn). Cambridge: Cambridge University Press.

Ekman, P. & Friesen, W.V. (1969). The repertoire of nonverbal behavior: Categories, origins, usage, and coding. *Semiotica*, **1**, 49–67.

Ekman, P. & Friesen, W.V. (1975). *Unmasking the Face*. Englewood Cliffs, NJ: Prentice Hall.

Engholm, C. (1991). *When Business East meets Business West: The Guide to Practice and Protocol in the Pacific Rim*. New York: Wiley.

Ervin-Tripp, S.M. (1964). Language and TAT content in French–English bilinguals. *Journal of Abnormal and Social Psychology*, **68**, 500–507.

Ervin-Tripp, S.M. (1971). Sociolinguistics. In J.A. Fishman (Ed.), *Advances in the Sociology of Language* (Vol. 1, pp. 15–91). The Hague: Mouton.

Feldman, R.S. (Ed.) (1992). *Applications of Nonverbal Behavioral Theories and Research*. Hillsdale, NJ: Lawrence Erlbaum.

Fishman, J.A. (1971a). *Sociolinguistics: A Brief Introduction*. Rowley, MA: Newbury House.

Fishman, J.A. (1971b). The sociology of language: An interdisciplinary social science approach to language in society. In J.A. Fishman (Ed.), *Advances in the Sociology of Language* (Vol. 1, pp. 217–404). The Hague: Mouton.

French, J. & Raven, B.H. (1959). The bases of social power. In D. Cartwright (Ed.), *Studies in Social Power*. Ann Arbor, MI: Institute for Social Research.

Furnham, A. (1983). Situational determinants of social skill. In R. Ellis & D. Whittington (Eds), *New Directions in Social Skills Training* (pp. 77–114). London: Croom Helm.

Gallois, C. (1993). The language and communication of emotion: Universal, interpersonal, or intergroup? *American Behavioral Scientist*, **36**, 262–270.

Gallois, C. & Callan, V.J. (1981). Personality impressions elicited by accented English speech. *Journal of Cross-Cultural Psychology*, **12**, 347–359.

Gallois, C. & Callan, V.J. (1986). Decoding emotional messages: Influence of ethnicity, sex, message type, and channel. *Journal of Personality and Social Psychology*, **51**, 755–762.

Gallois, C. & Callan, V.J. (1988). Communication and the prototypical speaker: Predicting evaluations of status and solidarity. *Language and Communication*, **8**, 271–283.

Gallois, C. & Callan, V.J. (1991). Interethnic accommodation: The role of norms. In H. Giles, N. Coupland & J. Coupland (Eds), *Contexts of Accommodation: Developments in Applied Sociolinguistics* (pp. 245–269). Cambridge: Cambridge University Press.

Gallois, C., Callan, V.J. & McKenzie Palmer, J.A. (1992). The influence of applicant communication style and interviewer characteristics on hiring decisions. *Journal of Applied Social Psychology*, **22**, 1040–1059.

Gallois, C., Giles, H., Jones, E., Cargile, A.C. & Ota, H. (1995). Accommodating intercultural encounters: Elaborations and extensions. In R. Wiseman (Ed.), *Intercultural Communication Theory* (pp. 115–147). Thousand Oaks, CA: Sage.

Genesee, F. & Bourhis, R.Y. (1982). The social psychological significance of code switching in cross-cultural communication. *Journal of Language and Social Psychology*, **1**, 1–27.

Genesee, F. & Bourhis, R.Y. (1988). Evaluative reactions to language choice strategies: The role of sociocultural factors. *Language and Communication*, **8**, 229–250.

Giles, H. & Coupland, N. (1991). *Language: Contexts and Consequences*. Milton Keynes: Open University Press.

Giles, H. & Johnson, P. (1987). Ethnolinguistic identity theory: A social-psychological approach to language maintenance. *International Journal of the Sociology of Language*, **68**, 66–99.

Giles, H., Bourhis, R.Y. & Taylor, D.M. (1977). Towards a theory of language in ethnic group relations. In H. Giles (Ed.), *Language, Ethnicity and Intergroup Relations*. London: Academic Press.

Grice, P. (1975). Logic and conversation. In P. Cole & J. Morgan (Eds), *Syntax and Semantics 3: Speech Acts* (pp. 107–142). New York: Academic Press.

Gudykunst, W.B. (1991). *Bridging Differences: Effective Intergroup Communication*. Newbury Park, CA: Sage.

Gudykunst, W.B. (1995). Anxiety/uncertainty management (AUM) theory: Current status. In R.L. Wiseman (Ed.), *Intercultural Communication Theory* (pp. 8–58). Thousand Oaks, CA: Sage.

Gudykunst, W.B. & Ting-Toomey, S. (Eds) (1988). *Culture and Interpersonal Communication.* Newbury Park, CA: Sage.

Gudykunst, W.B., Matsumoto, Y., Ting-Toomey, S., Nishida, T., Kim, K. & Heyman, S. (1996). The influence of cultural individualism-collectivism, self-construals, and individual values on communication styles across cultures. *Human Communication Research*, **22**, 510–543.

Gumperz, J.J. (Ed.) (1982). *Discourse Strategies.* Cambridge: Cambridge University Press.

Hall, E.T. (1959). *The Silent Language.* Greenwich: Fawcett.

Hall, E.T. (1966). *The Hidden Dimension.* New York: Doubleday.

Hall, E.T. (1976). *Beyond Culture.* New York: Anchor Press/ Doubleday.

Hall, E.T. (1995). Communicating at the cultural interface between high and low context cultures. Paper presented at the Annual Conference of the International Communication Association, Albuquerque, NM, 25–29 May.

Hall, J.A. (1979). Gender, gender roles, and nonverbal communication skills. In R. Rosenthal (Ed.), *Skill in Nonverbal Communication: Individual Differences* (pp. 32–67). Cambridge. MA: Oelgeschlager, Gunn & Hain.

Harré, R. & Secord, P. (1972). *The Explanation of Social Behaviour.* Blackwell: Oxford.

Hayduk, L.A. (1978). Personal space: An evaluative and orienting overview. *Psychological Bulletin*, **85**, 117–134.

Hayduk, L.A. (1983). Personal space: Where we now stand. *Psychological Bulletin*, **94**, 293–335.

Henley, N.M. (1977). *Body Politics: Power, Sex, and Nonverbal Communication.* Englewood Cliffs, NJ: Prentice Hall.

Henley, N.M. & Kramarae, C. (1991). Gender, power and miscommunication. In N. Coupland, H. Giles & J.M. Wiemann (Eds), *Miscommunication and Problematic Talk* (pp. 18–43). Newbury Park, CA: Sage.

Hewstone, M. & Brown, R. (1986). Contact is not enough: An intergroup perspective on the 'Contact Hypothesis'. In M. Hewstone & R. Brown (Eds), *Contact and Conflict in Intergroup Encounters* (pp. 1–44). Oxford: Basil Blackwell.

Hildebrandt, N. & Giles, H. (1983). The Japanese as subordinate group: ethnolinguistic identity theory in a foreign language context. *Anthropological Linguistics*, **25**, 436–466.

Hofstede, G. (1980). *Culture's Consequences: International Differences in Work-related Values.* Beverly Hills: Sage.

Hofstede, G. (1983). Dimensions of national cultures in fifty countries and three regions. In J. Deregowski, S. Dzuirawiec & R. Annis (Eds), *Explicitations in Cross-cultural Psychology* (pp. 335–355). Lisse, Switzerland: Swets & Zeitlinger.

Hogg, M. & Abrams, D. (1988). *Social Identifications: A Social Psychology of Intergroup Relations and Group Processes.* London: Routledge.

Horvath, B.M. (1985). *Variations in Australian English: The Sociolects of Sydney.* Melbourne: Cambridge University Press.

Hrop, S. & Rakos, R.F. (1985). The influence of race in the social evaluation of assertion in conflict situations. *Behavior Therapy,* **16,** 478–493.

Jones, E., Gallois, C., Callan, V.J. & Barker, M. (1994). Evaluations of interactions between students and academic staff: Influence of communication accommodation, ethnic group, and status. *Journal of Language and Social Psychology,* **13,** 158–191.

Jones, E., Gallois, C., Callan, V.J. & Barker, M. (1995). Language and power in an academic context: The effects of status, ethnicity, and sex. *Journal of Language and Social Psychology,* **14,** 434–461.

Joos, M. (1962). The five clocks. *International Journal of American Linguistics,* **28,** part V.

Jourard, S.M. (1966). An exploratory study of body accessibility. *British Journal of Social and Clinical Psychology,* **5,** 221–231.

Kashima, Y., Yamaguchi, S., Kim, U., Choi, S.-H., Gelfand, M.J. & Yuki, M. (1995). Culture, gender, and self: A perspective from the individualism–collectivism research. *Journal of Personality and Social Psychology,* **69,** 925–937.

Kayany, J.M., Wotring, C.E. & Forrest, E.J. (1996) Relational control and interactive media choice in technology-mediated communication situations. *Human Communication Research,* **22,** 371–398.

Kim, Y.Y. (1988). *Communication and Cross-cultural Adaptation: An Integrative Theory.* Clevedon: Multilingual Matters.

Kim, Y.Y. (1995). Cross-cultural adaptation: An integrative theory. In R.L. Wiseman (Ed.), *Intercultural Communication Theory* (pp. 170–193). Thousand Oaks, CA: Sage.

Lambert, W.E., Havelka, J. & Crosby, C. (1959). The influence of language-acquisition contexts on bilingualism. *Journal of Abnormal and Social Psychology,* **56,** 239–244.

Lambert, W.E., Hodgson, R.C., Gardner, R.C. & Fillenbaum, S. (1960). Evaluational reactions to spoken languages. *Journal of Abnormal and Social Psychology,* **66,** 44–51.

Lange, A.J. & Jakubowski, P. (1976). *Responsible Assertive Behavior.* IL: Research Press.

Lanzetta, J.T., Cartwright-Smith, J. & Kleck, R.E. (1976). Effects of nonverbal dissimulation on emotional experience and autonomic arousal. *Journal of Personality and Social Psychology*, **33**, 354–370.

Lippmann, W. (1922). *Public Opinion*. New York: Harcourt.

Lutz, C.A. (1990). Engendered emotion: Gender, power, and the rhetoric of emotional control in American discourse. In C.A. Lutz & L. Abu-Lughod (Eds), *Language and the Politics of Emotion* (pp. 69–91). Cambridge and Paris: Cambridge University Press and Edition de la Maison des Sciences de l'Homme.

Mark, N. (1995). From Oh No to OK: Communicating with your international teaching assistant. Paper presented at the Annual Conference of the International Communication Association, Albuquerque, NM, 25–29 May.

Markus, H.R. & Kitayama, S. (1991). Culture and the self: Implications for cognition, emotion, and motivation. *Psychological Review*, **98**, 224–253.

Markus, H.R. & Kitayama, S. (1994). *Emotion and Culture: Empirical Studies of Mutual Influence*. Washington, DC: American Psychological Association.

Matsumoto, D. (1994). Culture and emotion. In L.L. Adler & U.P. Gielen (Eds), *Cross-cultural Topics in Psychology* (pp. 115–124). Westport, CT: Greenwood.

McLuhan, M. (1964). *Understanding Media*. New York: McGraw-Hill.

Morris, D., Collett, P., Marsh, P. & O'Shaugnessy, M. (1979). *Gestures: Their Origins and Distribution*. New York: Stein & Day.

Ng, S.H. & Bradac, J.J. (1993). *Power in Language*. Newbury Park, CA: Sage.

Noller, P. (1984). *Nonverbal Communication and Marital Interaction*. Oxford: Pergamon.

Noller, P. & Gallois, C. (1986). Sending emotional messages in marriage: Non-verbal behaviour, sex and communication clarity. *British Journal of Social Psychology*, **25**, 287–297.

O'Sullivan, K. (1994). *Understanding Ways: Communicating between Cultures*. Sydney: Hale & Iremonger.

Oakes, P.J., Haslam, A.S. & Turner, J.C. (1994). *Stereotyping and Social Reality*. Oxford: Blackwell.

Osgood, C.E., May, W.H. & Miron, M.S. (1975). *Cross-cultural Universals of Affective Meaning*. Urbana: University of Illinois Press.

Pearce, P.L. (1982). *The Social Psychology of Tourist Behaviour*. Oxford: Pergamon.

Pittam, J. (1994). *Voice in Social Interaction: An Interdisciplinary Approach*. Thousand Oaks, CA: Sage.

Pittam, J. & Gallois, C. (1996). Communication attitudes and accommodation in Australia: A culturally diverse English-dominant context. *International Journal of Psycholinguistics*, **12**, 193–212.

Rakos, R.F. (1991). *Assertive Behavior: Theory, Research and Training*. London: Routledge.

Ramsay, S., Gallois, C. & Callan, V.J. (in press). Social rules held by personnel officers in job interviews: Impact on impressions and hiring. *Journal of Organisational and Occupational Psychology*.

Rao, N. (1995). The Oh No! syndrome: A language expectation model of undergraduates' negative reactions toward foreign teaching assistants. Paper presented at the Annual Conference of the International Communication Association, Albuquerque, NM, 25–29 May.

Riggio, R.E. (1986). Assessment of basic social skills. *Journal of Personality and Social Psychology*, **51**, 649–660.

Rintel, S. & Pittam, J. (1997). Strangers in a strange land: Managing interaction on internet relay chat. *Human Communication Research*, **24**(4).

Robinson, G.L. (1988). *Cross-cultural Understanding*. Sydney: Prentice Hall.

Rosenthal, R. (Ed.) (1979). *Skill in Nonverbal Communication: Individual Differences*. Cambridge, MA: Oelgeschlager, Gunn & Hain.

Rosenthal, R., Hall, J.A., DiMatteo, M.R., Rogers, P.L. & Archer, D. (1978). *Sensitivity to Nonverbal Communication: The PONS Test*. Baltimore: Johns Hopkins University Press.

Ross, S. & Shortreed, I.M. (1990). Japanese foreigner talk: Convergence or divergence? *Journal of Asian Pacific Communication*, **1**, 134–145.

Rubin, D. (1995). Undergraduates' perceptions of European vs. Asian instructors: Further studies of language and attitude in higher education. Paper presented at the Annual Conference of the International Communication Association, Albuquerque, NM, 25–29 May.

Rubin, J. (1970). Bilingual usage in Paraguay. In J.A. Fishman (Ed.), *Readings in the Sociology of Language* (pp. 512–530). The Hague: Mouton.

Russell, J.A. (1991). Culture and the categorization of emotions. *Psychological Bulletin*, **110**, 426–450.

Ryan, E.B. & Giles, H. (Eds) (1982). *Attitudes towards Language Variation: Social and Applied Contexts*. London: Edward Arnold.

Ryan, E.B., Giles, H. & Sebastian, R.J. (1982). An integrative perspective for the study of attitudes towards language variation. In E.B. Ryan & H. Giles (Eds), *Attitudes towards Language Variation: Social and Applied Contexts*. London: Edward Arnold.

Sachdev, I., Bourhis, R.Y., Phang, S.-W. & D'Eye, J. (1987). Language attitudes and vitality perceptions: Intergenerational effects among Chinese Canadian communities. *Journal of Language and Social Psychology*, **6**, 287–308.

Scherer, K.R. (1979). Personality markers in speech. In K.R. Scherer & H. Giles (Eds), *Social Markers in Speech* (pp. 147–209). New York: Cambridge University Press.

Scherer, K.R. (1988). *Facets of Emotion: Recent Research*. Hillsdale, NJ: Lawrence Erlbaum.

Scott, W.A. & Scott, R. (1989). *Adaptation of Immigrants: Individual Differences and Determinants*. Oxford: Pergamon.

Seggie, I., Fulmizi, C. & Stewart, J. (1982). Evaluation of personality traits and employment suitability based on various Australian accents. *Australian Journal of Psychology*, **34**, 345–357.

Semin, G.R. & Fiedler, K. (Eds) (1992). *Language, Interaction and Social Cognition*. London: Sage.

Shockley-Zalabak, P. (1991). *Fundamentals of Organizational Communication: Knowledge, Sensitivity, Skills, Values* (2nd edn). New York: Longman.

Sias, P.M. & Jablin, F.M. (1995). Differential superior–subordinate relations, perceptions of fairness, and coworker communication. *Human Communication Research*, **22**, 5–38.

Singelis, T.M. & Brown, W.J. (1995). Culture, self, and collectivist communication: Linking culture to individual behavior. *Human Communication Research*, **21**, 354–389.

Smolicz, J.J. (1979). *Culture and Education in a Plural Society*. Canberra: Curriculum Development Centre.

Sommer, R. (1969). *Personal Space: The Behavioral Basis of Design*. Englewood Cliffs, NJ: Prentice Hall.

Sparks, B.A. (1995). Communication and the service encounter. Unpublished PhD thesis, The University of Queensland, Brisbane, Australia.

St Lawrence, J.S., Hansen, D.J., Cutts, T.F., Tisdelle, D.A. & Irish, J.D. (1985). Situational context: Effects of perceptions of assertive and unassertive behavior. *Behavior Therapy*, **16**, 51–62.

Tajfel, H. (1979). Individuals and groups in social psychology. *British Journal of Social and Clinical Psychology*, **18**, 183–190.

Tajfel, H. & Turner, J.C. (1979). An integrative theory of intergroup conflict. In W.G. Austin & S. Worchel (Eds), *The Social Psychology of Intergroup Relations*. Monterey, CA: Brooks/Cole.

Tannen, D. (1986). *That's Not What I Meant!* New York: Ballantine.

Tannen, D. (1990). *You Just Don't Understand!* New York: Morrow.

Taylor, D.M. & McKirnan, D.J. (1984). A five-stage model of intergroup relations. *British Journal of Social Psychology*, **23**, 291–300.

Trudgill, P. (1986). *Dialects in Contact.* New York: Basil Blackwell.

Turner, J.C. (Ed.) (1987). *Rediscovering the Social Group: A Self-Categorization Theory.* New York: Basil Blackwell.

Vaughan, G.M. & Hogg, M.A. (1995). *Introduction to Social Psychology.* Sydney: Prentice Hall.

Willemyns, M., Gallois, C., Callan V.J. & Pittam, J. (1997). Accent accommodation in the job interview: Impact of sex and interviewer accent. *Journal of Language and Social Psychology,* **16.**

Wilson, K. & Gallois, C. (1993). *Assertion and its Social Context.* London: Pergamon.

Wilson, K., Whicker, L. & Price, L. (1994). Social rules for interpersonally effective behaviour in conflict situations. Paper presented at the Fifth International Conference on Language and Social Psychology, Brisbane, Australia, 6–9 July.

Wolpe, J. (1958). *Psychotherapy by Reciprocal Inhibition.* Stanford, CA: Stanford University Press.

Zajonc, R.B., Murphy, S.T. & Inglehart, M. (1989). Feeling and facial efference: Implications of the vascular theory of emotion. *Psychological Review,* **96,** 395–416.

Ziff, L. (Ed.) (1982) *Ralph Waldo Emerson: Selected Essays.* Harmondsworth: Penguin.

# AUTHOR INDEX

# SUBJECT INDEX

# Related titles of interest from Wiley...

## Culture and the Child

**A Guide for Professionals in Child Care and Development**

**Daphne Keats**

Relates cultural differences in development to the problems and practice of child care with a special contribution from cross-cultural psychology.

**Wiley Series in Culture and Professional Practice**

0-471-96625-8   160pp   1997   Paperback

## Handbook of Work and Health Psychology

Edited by **Marc J. Schabracq, Jacques A.M. Winnubst** and **Cary L. Cooper**

Explores a range of topics linking the two fields of work and health psychology.

0-471-95789-5   512pp   1996   Hardback

## Handbook of Work Group Psychology

Edited by **Michael West**

Provides a comprehensive, critical and up-to-date overview of all the key areas of group psychology in the context of organizational and work groups.

0-471 95790-9   642pp   1996   Hardback

## Black in White

**The Caribbean Child in the UK Home**

**Jean Harris Hendriks** and **John Figueroa**

This thought-provoking book addresses sensitive issues affecting Carribean children growing up in the UK, drawing on the authors' experience of child psychiatry, adoption and fostering, education, welfare systems and the law.

0-471-97224-X   154pp   1995   Paperback

---

Visit the Wiley Home Page at http://www.wiley.co.uk